WHAT IS CREATIVE THINKING?

What Is Creative Thinking?

BY

CATHARINE PATRICK, Ph.D.

PHILOSOPHICAL LIBRARY
NEW YORK

TO
ELMER B. HODGES, LL.B.

CONTENTS

All
Body

INTRODUCTION

THE progress of civilization is marked by its milestones of the great discoveries and inventions. The masterpieces in the art museums, the great plays and novels, the music of the orchestra and the opera, the solutions of complicated mathematical and astronomical problems, the discoveries in the chemical laboratories, the airplanes and electrical appliances are all the results of creative thinking.

What is the nature of this mental process, which typically precedes all the outstanding achievements made by man? What are the characteristics of creative thought? What are the stages in our thinking? What do we mean by "inspiration"? Does the creative thinking of the ordinary person show the same essential structure as that of the famous artist, scientist, or inventor?

Although we recognize many and wide differences between a Shakespearean play, an American folk song, the chemical formula for radium, and a formulated legal cause yet the process of thinking which preceded the production of these diverse products exhibited the same essential stages in each instance. The methods, materials, and aims may vary greatly in the various fields of human endeavor, but the psychological process underlying the production of a work of art, or an invention, or a law, or a scientific formula is fundamentally the same in all cases.

Can anything be done to stimulate creative thinking, so that we may reap the benefits of more original ideas? This is the problem which confronts us in every field of human endeavor. What changes need to be made in the curricula of the schools and colleges to promote more productive thinking? Similarly, what changes need to be made in the working and living habits of adults? By removing unfavorable conditions and providing additional opportunities, we can do much to encourage and foster creative thought.

In order to meet this challenge it is imperative to have adequate knowledge about productive thinking. The aim of this book is to present in one volume the available information about creative thinking, which now is scattered among a number of articles and chapters of various books. We aim to bring together the viewpoints and investigations of many different writers within the covers of one volume, so that the reader may get a comprehensive view of the whole field of creative thought, as well as the individual contributions.

In the wide field of education extending throughout this country more emphasis is constantly being placed on affording additional opportunities for creative activities on the part of pupils and students in both rural and urban institutions. More and more teachers realize the importance of providing additional outlets for creative thinking along the lines of the pupils' special interests and aptitudes. The teacher and educator will find that a better understanding of the nature of the creative process, as provided by this book, is helpful in planning courses of study and curricula, whether at the elementary or high school level.

The way the mind works to produce great works of art and important inventions is a topic which stimulates the curiosity and interest of all students of psychology. They will find it highly useful in courses which stress thinking. The research psychologist will appreciate the convenience of having descriptions, definitions, and results of investigations in creative thought combined in one volume

Not only those who work in education and psychology, but also students of aesthetics, literature and art will derive benefit from this book.

Aesthetics is chiefly concerned with the problem of the

nature of art in all the forms and mediums in which it occurs. One of the fundamental questions to be answered in any course in aesthetics, literature and art is that of the nature of creative thought. The student is immediately confronted with the question, "How was that art produced?" "What is creative thinking?" This volume, with its comprehensive survey of the psychological descriptions and explanations of creative thought, will afford the necessary information.

The amateur psychologist among the general public will welcome this book as an addition to his library. Certain chapters will especially appeal to him as those which describe the stages of thought, emotion in creative thinking, the ages of greatest achievement, and how he can improve conditions so that he and others may do more creative work. He will find much to interest him in the accounts from the actual experiences of thinkers.

The purpose of this book is to present the viewpoints of various authors and investigators so that the reader can gain an understanding of the contribution made by each one. From a comparison of the many different definitions and descriptions which have been offered, he may obtain a comprehensive evaluation of the whole field. We have attempted a critical evaluation of the various statements in order to bring out the essential nature of creative thinking. Attention has been given to the conditions which facilitate creative thought, as well as to those which hinder its development. We have pointed out suggested changes in educational procedures and the mode of living of adults to favor more productive thought.

WHAT IS CREATIVE THINKING?

1

PREPARATION

THE great advance of civilization through the centuries has depended on creative thinking. It is the basic process underlying all the important inventions and discoveries. Literature, music, painting, sculpture, drama, and all other forms of art depend on creative thinking.

If we stop for a moment and think what life would be without the comforts of civilization, we immediately become aware of the vital importance of creative thinking. If for a minute we imagine ourselves living in a world without culture, we realize the immense importance of creative thought. If we think of any large city, and then imagine for a moment the appearance of the landscape if the city were nonexistent and had vanished, we comprehend the large significance of creative thinking.

We all at one time or another have wondered how a certain work of art, an invention, or a scientific discovery was made. Each of us has asked that question at one time or another. We marvel at the excellence of the product and wonder how it was conceived. We wonder how the writer, artist, musician, inventor, or scientist thought to produce the great work of literature, music, art or the new invention.

Creative thinking of longer or shorter duration is behind every great work of art or science and behind every invention, which has advanced the progress of civilization. Without creative thinking there would be no progress in civilization. Without creative thinking we would have none of the luxuries and comforts of modern life.

Creative thought is characterized by the four stages of preparation, incubation, illumination, and revision or verification. The first stage is preparation. Let us now turn to an examination of that first stage.

The First Stage

Preparation is the first stage in the creative thought process. "I want to find out all I can about this problem," says the thinker to himself. "I want to get an idea for my poem (or picture or musical composition)," or "I want to collect all the scientific data which has been done on this problem," are typical sentences describing the type of mental activity during this stage.

The physicist Helmholtz, on the occasion of his seventieth birthday, was asked by friends to describe how he made his great discoveries. He said that after previous investigation of the problem "in all directions . . . happy ideas came unexpectedly without effort like inspiration. . . . It was always requisite that I should have turned my problem over on all sides, hither and thither, to the point where I could see all its turns and complexities in my head and could run through them freely without writing. To bring matters to this point is usually impossible without long preparatory labor." Helmholtz thus distinguishes the first stage of creative thought.

In his essay on creative thought Ribot writes, "One of the best conditions for inventing is an abundance of material, accumulated experience. . . . The revelations of inventors or of their biographers leave no doubt as to the necessity of a large number of sketches, trials, preliminary drawings, no matter whether it is a matter of industry, commerce, a machine, a poem, an opera, a picture, a building, a plan of campaign." The first requirement for finding something new is "to be fertile in hypotheses. . . . We seldom find ideas exactly what we want."

The gifted mathematician Poincare describes this first stage of his work on a difficult problem: "I had been endeavoring for two weeks to demonstrate that there could be no function analogous to those I have since called functions fuchsiennes. Each day for fifteen days I spent an hour or two at the work table" but with no solution. He tried a great number of combinations. He adds that "sudden inspirations never happen except after some days of voluntary effort which has appeared absolutely fruitless and whence nothing good seems to have come, where the way taken seems totally astray. . . . Often when a man is working at a difficult question, he accomplishes nothing the first time he sets to work. Then he takes more or less of a rest and sits down again at his table."

Woodworth points out that "the stages noted by Helmholtz and Poincare are familiar to many solvers of original problems. First they 'load up' with all available information and make determined efforts to reach a prompt solution; and sometimes they are successful in this first heat." But often days or weeks elapse before the saving idea comes.

"This bringing forth of inventions, solutions, and discoveries rarely occurs except to a mind that has previously steeped itself consciously in material relating to its question," writes Dewey. Christof notes that the first phase, which is the "formulation of the problem," involves bafflement and search. The issue that the person faces is defined, restated, brought into relation with other presumably pertinent matters, and carried to the point where familiarity with the area is much greater than it was at the very start according to Hartmann. Thus preparation precedes the other stages in Prescott's opinion.

The kind of information which a person collects in this first stage has an important bearing on the way he finally solves the problem. In fact, Downey writes that "all so-called inspirations occur strictly within the limit of the individual's capacity, training, and previous cogitations." Szekely states that there is a functional relation between knowledge or previous experience and productive, creative thinking. Gesell brings out a similar point of view when he says, "Genius may have effortless moments, . . . these moments are usually preceded by prolonged periods of preparation. The so-called unconscious cerebration can take place only as a result of purposeful endeavor. . . . The scientific genius is a prodigious worker endowed with persevering patience."

Duncker says, "The deliberating and searching is always confined to a province which is relatively narrow as to space and content. Thus preparation is made for the more discrete phases of a solution by certain *approximate regional demarcations,* i.e. by phases in which necessary but not yet sufficient properties of the solution are demanded. Such implicit phases of a solution do not quite fulfill even the first prerequisite of a solution. . . . Now since each aspect of the premises, in and for itself, could be the origin of some solution—and several such aspects dealt with successively that much more—the subject must be just so much better off, the more and the more varied aspects he is able to command at one glance, i.e. without tedious 'work of explication.' . . . The one-sidedness, the poverty of aspect of thought material is—as we shall in every case distinctly observe—the chief characteristic of poor thinking."

Preparation May be Deliberate or Nondeliberate

Collecting information in preparation may be either deliberate or nondeliberate. Shaffer, Gilmer and Schoen have presented a good description of the way in which people in this stage gain knowledge of the problems they want to solve. "In scientific discovery, deliberate preparation is most frequent. The research worker studies the tools essential to his problem, and reads the previous contributions to his field of study. Before becoming a discoverer he must first become a scholar. Nondeliberate preparation may often play an important part, however. A man who has abandoned the field of physics to take up the study of psychology may later find that his knowledge of physics is the key to an important contribution to his newer area of interest. In fact, a characteristic of a creative thinker is his ability to combine and apply experiences that originally were gained at various times and for diverse purposes. In painting and music, deliberate preparation is important, for a mastery of techniques is a prerequisite to the invention of new effects and combinations.

"Undeliberated preparation for creative work is seen most clearly in literature, especially in poetry. Many writers have kept notebooks in which they jotted down observations, chance thoughts, and bits of fact or style culled from their reading. In Coleridge's notebook, for example, may be found the germs of *The Ancient Mariner* and *Kubla Khan*. Coleridge, an omnivorous reader, assimilated the traditions and folk stories of the Far East, the superstitions of the Middle Ages, the habits of the albatross, lore about sailors and boats, and the plots of ancient Greek legends. From this heterogeneous mass of material sprang his great imaginative poems. He was not gathering material for a planned poem when he read. Instead, the material was acquired randomly and for its own sake. Only after the preparation was complete did Coleridge conceive the poems, with that ability to recombine that is a mark of genius."

Carpenter described the type of activity which occurs in the preparation stage in his report of Mr. Appold, inventor of the centrifugal pump. "It was his habit, when a difficulty arose, carefully to consider the exact result he required; and having satisfied himself upon that point, he would direct his attention to the simplest mode in which the end could be obtained. With that in view, he would during the day bring together in his mind all the facts and principles relating to the case, and the solution of the problem usually occurred to him in the early morning after sleep."

Speaking of "the reception of the data" as the first stage, Feibleman says, "It should be stressed, however, that the imagination of the artist is a faculty which is already present in his reception of the data that come to him from the external world. The apprehension of sense impressions is in one way a passive process. . . . The mind of the artist is a sensitive mechanism like a photographic plate which receives, enters, stores, and records the impressions made upon it by the phenomena of the external world. In quite another way, however, the apprehension of sense impressions is active. For the mind is able to select that part of the external world from which it wishes to receive its sense impressions. We are able to focus the camera containing the photographic plate upon any object we choose. It is in this latter, active connection that the imagination of the artist already plays a part."

In this first stage the thinker may spend many hours reading books and articles on the same general topic and making memoranda of the chief points. He might also spend as much time reading opposing kinds of work to obtain different viewpoints. Or, instead of reading, he might find it more profitable to talk with several people who were well informed. As Platt and Baker conclude from replies obtained from several hundred research workers and directors of research, "the mind must be well provided with facts."

"Before anyone could give himself up to inspiration he must have acquired a mastery over his subject in order that the technical aspects should be in no way a hindrance to him," asserts Harding. "New discoveries and inventions resulting, as they frequently do, from a coalition of ideas from widely different subjects, knowledge outside and beyond the chosen profession is a considerable asset towards the achievement of the new and original." Many persons who attained distinction in later life practised their vocation in childhood, and had standards of culture unusually wide.

Attitude of Doubt and Perplexity

Preparation is characterized by an attitude of doubt and uncertainty. Hutchinson points out it is a period of "trial and error activity." There is random effort with false starts on the basis of inadequate hypotheses. Stereotyped errors and a sense of frustration are characteristic. Dewey shows that reflective thought begins with a state of doubt, which is characterized by hesitation and perplexity. "After prolonged preoccupation with an intellectual topic the mind ceases to function readily. It has apparently got into a rut; the wheels go round in the head; but they do not turn out any fresh grist. New suggestions cease to occur. The mind is . . . fed up." Likewise Christof points out that thinking begins in bafflement and search for the significance of an obscure and puzzling situation. This first stage is accompanied by an attitude of doubt.

Length of Stage

The period of preparation may last minutes or hours or consume months or years. In his scholarly book, *Road to Xanadu,* Lowes describes how Coleridge spent years reading and jotting down notes about the tales and legends of the sea. "One after another vivid bits from what he had read dropped into that deep well," resulting in the production of poems, as *The Ancient Mariner.* Or a poet may spend a relatively short time searching for ideas in writing a lyric poem. The author of a historical novel may read for a long time to collect relevant material. A lawyer may work hard reading similar cases. A mathematician or scientist may work for months to obtain adequate information about a problem he wishes to solve. The length of this stage for one mathematician is seen in the following quotation from Poincare. "These sudden inspirations never happen except after some days of voluntary effort, which has appeared absolutely fruitless." Wallas notes this variation in the length of time consumed when he says preparation may last a few seconds or several

hours or longer periods than that. The acquisition of technical habits in this first stage may involve years, as Hutchinson
has pointed out.

Preparation is the period when the subject is assembling
or receiving new ideas. During this time the associations shift
rapidly. One's ideas are not yet dominated by any coherent
theme or formulation. It is a time when new thoughts seem
to be "pressing in upon the mind," as one writer expressed it.
A poet gazes at a landscape or sunset and receives various impressions of it. A mathematician starts to solve a problem and
considers its various phases. In order to study this stage, as
well as those of incubation, illumination, and verification,
Patrick studied the writing of poetry under laboratory conditions in order that the actual development of poems might
be observed. In this way it was believed that more could be
learned of the essentials of the process than by relying on the
analysis of written documents, biographies, and clinical evidence, as other investigators have done.

One hundred and thirteen persons took part in an experiment and were divided into two groups, an "experimental
group" of fifty-five poets, and a "control group" of fifty-eight
non-poets. The experimental group was composed only of
poets of ability whose work had appeared in the better poetry
magazines. Some of them were writers who were nationally
known, and who had already published volumes of well-
recognized poetry.

The group of poets were compared with a control group
composed of fifty-eight persons who were not writing poetry
and had never written any, except possibly as school assignments in their high school days. It was considered if they had
only written several poems as school assignments ten or
twenty years ago, and had not written any since, that the
effect of such small training would be negligible. A variety
of occupations was represented.

An individual interview was held with each person,
which began with a preliminary conversation, the chief pur-

pose of which was to enable the poet to become accustomed to talking aloud. After the poet had become accustomed to the situation, he was presented with a picture of a landscape, which included a variety of objects, and told to write a poem.

A record was kept of everything that was spoken from the moment of presenting the picture until the poet announced that the poem was completely finished, and needed no more revision. The creative process which the poets experience in their usual work is demonstrated in the creative process studied in this experiment. The four stages of creative thinking are evident. There was individual variation in time spent.

Summary

[During preparation, the first stage of creative thought, the thinker aims to acquire more information about the problem than he already possesses. In this period the ideas shift rapidly. One's thoughts are not yet dominated by any coherent theme or formulation. Reading in the field of the problem is an important method of acquiring more information, as well as discussion and communication with others doing the same type of work. The thinker's past experiences in the same or allied fields, as well as careful observation of one's present environment, are other sources.] Preparation may involve both deliberate and nondeliberate mental activity. Sometimes ideas seem to be pressing in upon the mind without much effort on the part of the subject, as in the case of the poet or artist who attempts to produce a work of art. On the other hand, the scientist or inventor may spend hours in strenuous mental effort to collect more information about his problem. This stage is typically accompanied by an unpleasant feeling state. It is often characterized by an attitude of doubt or perplexity. A sense of frustration is common, especially after long periods of preparation without reaching the solution. While short periods of preparation may be continuous, longer ones must necessarily be broken up by the routine of daily living. The stage of preparation may vary in length from a few minutes, as in the case of lyric poetry, to months or years, as in the preparation for an invention or a crucial experiment. Preparation is typically followed by incubation, although the two stages may overlap.

2

INCUBATION

The Second Stage

INCUBATION is the second stage in the creative thought process. After a person has struggled to solve a problem without success during the preparation stage, he frequently stops working on it for a while. He engages in other activities as recreation, sleep, physical exercise or doing other kinds of work. As he is busy with these different activities, he may find himself at intervals thinking of an idea which eventually leads to the solution. Each time this idea recurs to him it is modified until it is more clearly defined at the end of the stage than at the beginning and the solution is finally reached in the third stage of illumination.

The existence of this second stage of incubation in creative thought has been pointed out by various writers. In his essay written some years ago Ribot stated that inspiration signifies unconscious imagination and is the result of an underhand process existing in men. The "germ" is the first idea that strikes one after observing and studying. One brings to the solution all the materials gathered. There is a flowering; "when this latent work is sufficiently complete, the idea suddenly bursts forth."

The personal experiences of a gifted mathematician show how an idea about the solution may occur to a person after he has stopped actively working on a problem.

Poincare tried a great number of combinations to solve a problem and reached no results. He writes, "One evening, contrary to my custom, I drank black coffee and could not sleep. Ideas rose in crowds; I felt them collide until pairs interlocked, so to speak, making a stable combination. By the next morning I had established the existence of a class of Fuchsian functions, those which come from the hypergeometric series; I had only to write out the results, which took but a few hours." He describes his attempts to solve another problem when he says, "Then I turned my attention to the study of some arithmetical questions, apparently without much success and without a suspicion of any connection with my preceding researches. Disgusted with my failure, I went to spend a few days at the seaside, and thought of something else. One morning, walking on the bluff, the idea came to me with just the same characteristics of brevity, suddenness and immediate certainty that the arithmetic transformations of indeterminate ternary, quadratic forms were identical with those of non-Euclidean geometry."

"After the mind has ceased to be intent on the problem, and consciousness has relaxed its strain, a period of incubation sets in. The material rearranges itself; facts and principles fall into place; what was confused becomes bright and clear; the mixed up becomes orderly, often to such an extent that the problem is essentially solved," according to Dewey.

Platt and Baker have pointed out that the "mind must be well provided with facts, but periods of rest or temporary abandonment of a problem are quite essential. . . . A scientific hunch is a unifying or clarifying idea which springs into consciousness suddenly as a solution to a problem in which we are intensely interested. In typical cases it follows a long study, but comes into consciousness at a time when we are not working on the problem."

During this incubation stage, even though a person has quit trying to solve his problem for a while, "gradually an idea grows, annexing or using its neighbors, and becomes a mastering purpose which cannot be resisted. Finally it results in some creation," writes Dimnet. "The word 'incubation' rather implies the theory of unconscious work on a problem during a period of attention to other matters, but we can strip off this implication and use it simply to denote the fact —so far as it is a fact—that a period of inattention to a problem intervenes after preparation and before illumination. . . . Since the problem does *consciously recur* from time to time during the period of incubation, though without effortful work done upon it, partial solutions may be obtained," according to Woodworth.

Speaking from a practical point of view, Hartmann points out, "If the task is a long-drawn-out one, the incubation phase necessarily intervenes, because one has to be concerned with other life duties, even if these are no more serious than eating or sleeping. If the entire process is sharply telescoped, incubation as such may disappear; but in most extensive productions its chief function seems to be to restore the organism to a fresher and more zestful approach to the question that had earlier been carried to the point of fatigue or of ineffective work."

Relaxation or Activity Characterize this Stage

Physical exercise, rest, relaxation, recreation or different kind of mental work may characterize the incubation stage. Helmholtz describes his own personal experiences in physical exercise during this stage. He writes that after previous investigation of the problem "in all directions . . . happy ideas come unexpectedly without effort like inspiration. So far as I am concerned, they have never come to me when my mind was fatigued, or when I was at my working table. . . . They come particularly readily during the slow ascent of wooded hills on a sunny day. . . . It was always requisite that I should have turned my problem over on all sides, hither and thither, to the point where I could see all its turns and complexities in my head and could run through them freely, without writing. To bring matters to this point is usually impossible without long preparatory labor. In the next place, after the fatigue arising from this labor had passed away, there must come a time of bodily freshness and quiet well-being, before the good suggestions would occur. Often in exact agreement with Goethe's lines, they were there when I awoke of a morning. . . . But they came most readily . . . during leisurely walking over wooded hills in sunny weather. The smallest dose of alcohol seemed to scare them away."

Similarly A. E. Housman writes, "I would go out for a walk of two or three hours. As I went along, thinking of nothing in particular . . . there would flow into my mind, with sudden and unaccountable emotion, sometimes a line or two of verse, sometimes a whole stanza at once. . . . I happen to remember distinctly the genesis of the piece which stands last in my first volume. Two of the stanzas, I do not say which, came to my head, just as they are printed, while I was crossing the corner of Hampstead Heath between the Spaniard's Inn and the foot path to Temple Fortune. A third stanza came with a little coaxing after tea. One more was needed, but it did not come. I had to turn to and compose it myself and that was laborious business."

Meinicke tells of an engineer who had worked on a problem without success for a long time, and became tired and laid the problem aside. He was accustomed to take a walk along the river bank. There was a paddle steamboat, which he had been accustomed to see, but on a particular day there was also a new dredge. As he returned home past a bakery shop he received the successful idea for an invention, which combined the principles of the dredge and of the revolving paddle of the steamboat.

A person may rest or sleep during this second stage when he has temporarily quit working on a problem for a while. "Baffling problems are sometimes readily solved after an interval of rest, and this phenomenon is due in part to the fact that the problem is likely to be approached from a new intellectual standpoint," according to Carr. Also Harding suggests, "Absence of effort, passiveness and receptiveness were shown to be essential conditions of mind. . . . The decisive idea has the way of appearing when the mind is passive and even contemplating nothing in particular."

The kind of activity which may occur during the incubation stage varies for different people. Even the same person may show different behavior during this period on separate occasions. Wallas has said that this stage is composed of two factors: a. the "negative fact that during incubation we do not voluntarily or consciously think of a particular problem . . . b. the positive fact that a series of unconscious or involuntary (or foreconscious and forevoluntary) mental events take place then." The voluntary abstention from conscious thought has two forms: a. conscious mental work on some other problem. b. relaxation from all mental work. One can often "get more results in the same time by beginning several problems in succession and voluntarily leaving them unfinished while we turn to others, than by finishing work on each at one sitting." In the more difficult forms of creative thought we have an interval free of effort on it. For example, A. R. Wallace hit on the evolution theory in his berth during an attack of malaria at sea. Darwin on account of ill health spent much time in mental relaxation. A. Carrel got an important thought while walking in Brittany.

Carpenter had previously pointed out that "it is a common experience of inventors (whether artists, poets or mechanicians) that when they have been brought to a stand by some difficulty, the tangle will be more likely to unravel itself (so to speak) if the attention be completely withdrawn from it, than by any amount of continued effort. . . . They put it aside for a time and give their minds to something else, endeavoring to obtain either complete repose of mind, or refreshment by change of occupation, and they find that either after sleep, or after some period of recreation by a variety of employment, just what they want 'comes into their heads.' " He mentions a quotation by Abraham Tucker, as long ago as 1805, "With all our care to digest our materials, we cannot do it completely, but after a night's rest, or some recreation, or the mind being turned into some different course of thinking, she finds they have ranged themselves anew during her absence and in such manner as exhibits almost at one view all their mutual relations, dependencies and consequences."

Fehr investigated how scientists work and found that 75% acknowledge the appearance of discoveries while engaged upon subjects foreign to researches at the moment, while 90% often found it necessary to temporarily abandon important work. The problem shapes itself during the period of incubation. "This may be long or short, highly conscious or more indirective and random, and filled with experiences which are predominantly of either an emotional or intellectual nature," according to Commins.

Shaffer, Gilmer and Schoen have also pointed out that the behavior characteristic of the incubation period varies somewhat among persons and according to circumstances. One variety of incubation appears as restless and poorly coördinated activity.

"Incubation does not always occur in so obvious a form. It is sometimes reported that a scientist awakes from sleep with an inspiring solution of a perplexity, leading to the presumption that the incubation occurred during sleep. In other instances, the individual may turn to another task in the midst of which the answer to his previous problem will suddenly dawn on him. A vacation or period of relaxation will have the same effect, so that upon a return to work certain baffling difficulties are found to be clarified without deliberate effort. . . .

"The period of incubation gives rise to anecdotes about the absent-mindedness of creative thinkers. A chemist reported that on one morning he took a bath, shaved, and then took another bath. Only after the second bath did he realize that he had been concentrating on a problem for some time and that his reactions to his customary morning duties had been automatic and inattentive."

Feibleman mentions that if the artist does anything during incubation, "it tends to be something irrelevant, and often physical, and usually simple: fishing, sawing wood, or perhaps even desultory reading. From the public point of view it is a period of sterility because the audience is not able to detect in it any act of productivity by the artist. Lay persons are not able to see that this is in a way the artist's most productive time. For it is undoubtedly true that appearances are here deceiving."

Length of Stage

The length of this stage may range from minutes or hours to months or years. It varies from person to person, and also within the same individual from time to time. Rossman collected reports from inventors which show this variation in the length of time consumed. We quote some of the inventors' reports:

"I usually keep the thought or idea in mind as much as possible. This does not mean that I think of an idea continually, but I call it to mind as frequently as you would any subject that you were very much interested in, and, as the details of the idea take form, I make notes and sketches for reference. This may cover a period of from a few days to several years. Of course, if the time is long there may be periods of from several weeks to a couple of months' time that the idea is not called to mind, but when it is I always notice some progress during the interim." W. H. Wineman.

"First there must be a demand for the solution of some problem. Every conceivable method is then called to mind that will contribute to this solution. The problem is carried mentally for days. Now and then certain sketches will be

made. After the mental image is formed I go into the shop."
A. L. Collins.

The incubation period "may take months or even years,
taking it up and laying it down again a number of times—
then when alone and at rest the substantial invention suddenly appears to my mind." S. Olson.

Rossman concludes "when the problem is presented and
all the necessary data for its solution are marshalled a period
of incubation appears to be usually necessary. This may take
days or years. Many inventors relate they get their ideas when
they least expect them."

Portnoy quotes Amy Lowell as saying, "Long poems are
apt to take months preparing in the subconscious mind; in
the case of short poems the period of subconscious gestation
may be a day or an instant or any time between." He terms
incubation "a transitional stage during which the artist confines himself to routine matters of cleaning brushes, filling
in the detailed parts of an orchestration, rewriting old manuscripts."

Gesell describes the length of the incubation stage in the
case of Coleridge, who read copiously: "Long afterwards
these multifarious impressions, slumbering in the deep well,
came to concentrated confluence in forty-six words . . .
The 'Ancient Mariner' grew and grew, from November 13,
1797 to March 23, 1798." The growth had started before
that when Coleridge read in childhood.

The variation in the length of this stage is indicated by
Carpenter's quotation from a biography of Charlotte Bronte.
"She said that it was not every day that she could write. Sometimes weeks or even months elapsed before she felt that she
had anything to add to that portion of her story, which was
already written. Then, some morning she would waken up
and the progress of her tale lay clear and bright before her
in distinct vision, its incidents and consequent thoughts
being at such times more present to her mind than her actual
life itself."

The same thing is apparent in this quotation from Rimsky-Korsakoff which Rees presents: "I composed every day and all day; yet I managed to do much walking with my wife. . . . But musical thoughts and their fashioning pursued me persistently . . . the moods and contours of separate moments of the opera were outlining themselves in my conception. All of this was partly jotted down in the thick book, partly kept in my head . . . my fancy tended to . . . composing, and recording what I composed went very fast, now in the order of act and scene, and now by leaps, running ahead."

Rees also quotes Bennett as saying, "Today I spent such a day as ought to satisfy a man of letters. . . . At 2 I began, in my Bruges chair, to ponder further on my story, and the plot seemed to be coming. At 3:30 I made my afternoon tea, and then read more of Don Quixote, and fell asleep for about a minute. The plot was now coming faster and faster, and at 5 I decided that I would, at any rate, begin to sketch the story. At 6:45 I had done a complete rough draft of the whole story." During this stage the idea which is being incubated recurs spontaneously.

The incubation stage was studied in Patrick's experiment with poets mentioned in the preceding chapter. This was done by analyzing the written report obtained from each subject to see if an idea occurred early in the report, recurred one or more times, the subject meanwhile talking of other things, and at last appeared as the chief topic of the poem. Incubation does not differentiate the poets from the non-poets, but is apparently characteristic of the process of creative thinking. The data are in accord with the hypothesis that preparation leads to incubation.

Some of the statements regarding incubation, which were obtained from the poets by the aid of the questionnaire, are given below:

"A poem is a spiritual irritation. It annoys me till it breaks out. I sometimes incubate a mood for years. I do not

These differences in the length of the incubation
may be due to a number of factors. Some of these wo
the nature of the original stimulating situation and th
of problem the thinker is attempting to solve. The n
and intensity of the emotional reaction set up by the or
stimulus are contributing factors. The individual's per
habits and manner of living also exert influence. If a p
lem is very complex, certain aspects of it may be incub
longer than other aspects.

Idea Recurs Spontaneously

The idea or mood, which is incubated, recurs sponta
ously from time to time during this stage. Paulhan has no
a letter from Mozart, which includes the following quo
tion: "When I feel well and in a good humor, or when I a
taking a drive or walking after a good meal, or in the nigl
when I cannot sleep, thoughts crowd into my mind as easil
as you could wish. Whence and how do they come? . .
Those which please me, I keep in my head and hum them; a
least others have told me that I do so. Once I have my theme,
another melody comes, linking itself to the first one, in accordance with the needs of the composition as a whole: the
counterpoint, the part of each instrument, and all those
melodic fragments at last produce the entire work. Then my
soul is on fire with inspiration, if however nothing occurs to
distract my attention. The work grows; I keep expanding it,
conceiving it more and more clearly until I have the entire
composition finished in my head though it may be long."

The spontaneous recurrence of an idea during this stage
is evident in the following report presented by Rossman: "At
times ideas have bothered me for days and sometimes weeks
until I set to work them out to completion, and then found
that they amounted to invention. These are spontaneous
ideas beyond the control of the individual. . . . They occur at intervals of a few weeks to a number of months." T.
Appleby.

incubate the lines. The idea lies fallow and comes back when conditions are favorable."

"If I feel blue or excited, then I sit down and try to get it out of my system. Sometimes it grows for days and days, and I sit down and write it off. The mood comes first and then the phrase. Or I incubate the mood, then the phrase, then write the poem. I don't incubate lyrics long."

"First I have a mood, then I get two or three lines. Sometimes I carry those two or three lines around and sometimes not. A sudden stimulus starts the incubation of a poem, whether a mood or a line. A mood may lie fallow from a half hour to a year, then it comes back."

"I get a word and carry it around in my head. Then other words come. Pretty soon I get a phrase which is the nut of the poem, then I write the poem and modify that phrase."

"If I have a feeling for a poem I would read something that would keep the suggestion going and carry some sort of a living relation to me. For instance, when I wrote the poem, 'Morning Glories' the mood, as a sort of stillness, lasted for some time, and after a while the poem came to me. In this way ideas incubate."

The stage of incubation in scientific thinking was also investigated in another experiment by Patrick. One hundred people took part in this study and were divided into two groups of fifty each. One group planned a scientific experiment at one sitting; the other thought about it over a period of two or three weeks and kept a diary, in which they recorded any thoughts which they had concerning the problem during that time.

Incubation presents essentially the same characteristics, whether it only lasts a number of minutes or extends over a period of several weeks. This experiment on scientific thinking shows that the incubation, which only lasts a number of minutes, shows the same essential characteristics as that which continues several weeks.

Incubation has also been studied in the field of art. One

hundred persons took part in this investigation and were divided into two groups of fifty artists and fifty non-artists. The artists were persons of ability, whose work has appeared in the better exhibits.

The presence of incubation was shown if an idea occurred early in the report, recurred one or more times, the subject meanwhile talking of other things, and at last appeared as the chief topic of the picture. Incubation is characteristic of the thinking of both artists and non-artists.

Incubation follows preparation, although it may accompany it. We quote below some of the statements regarding incubation which were obtained from the artists by the aid of our questionnaire:

"I almost always carry an idea around a while in my mind before I start to work. It keeps coming back several times while I am doing other things, and I can work it out later. Sometimes I lose it if I don't work on it. In coming back it changes, and sometimes improves as it comes back. If I don't grab it, I may get something different."

"I incubate an idea for periods of two or three weeks. It may be for a month or more when I am not working on it. I think now of making a picture of Coconut Grove as it used to look, and I have been incubating that two years. Then I get to feel like I want to paint. I keep vaguely thinking of something like it to do. I am thinking now of a still life. This afternoon I may start on it. The idea recurs while I am doing other things, as I have thought of a still life for two or three weeks now. I think of the roundness of the fruit, and shapes against the glass bottle. It recurs in color, so when I am ready to paint I know what I want to do and do it very rapidly. A complicated thing becomes simple by thinking about it. I noticed a tree and did not think about it and before I knew it, I had all sorts of information for making it."

"I usually carry an idea around in my mind. I see the picture completely in my mind before I paint it. It recurs

from time to time and lasts a couple of weeks. I know the
color scheme before I start and get a model to fit that."

"One must put over to the observer what one sees. Often
I incubate an idea and it keeps recurring, as I saw children
in the north end of town, and the idea stayed with me until
painted a while later."

"I incubate an idea, as color and movement might interest me. It lasts a week only. It grows more intense till finished."

"I often carry an idea around for several weeks before I
make a picture though sometimes longer. I got ideas in
Santa Fe last summer to do now. The ideas recur from time
to time while I am occupied with other things."

Wertheimer in his book, "Productive Thinking," gives
a report of how he solved a mathematical problem. Although
an examination of his protocols shows that preparation and
incubation were present, he does not recognize the stages of
creative thought or mention them. We quote from one of his
protocols:

"During a conversation at lunch about ornaments, the
discussion touched on closed geometric figures such as tri-
angles, rectangles, hexagons, and other polygons. . . . In
the hours that followed, in which I had other things to do,
the problem continued to be active. After several hours it
had developed to this stage: There is, on the one hand, the
sum of the angles (A) in a figure; on the other hand, there is
the closed completeness (B) of the figure. Between A and B
there is only an 'and,' a simple conjunction. There is the one,
here is the other. This and-relationship between them is
somehow blind. What is really behind it all? What is the
trouble? The two must have something to do with each
other. It was not a feeling of two contradictory propositions.
I was directed toward the positive problem, 'How can I comprehend?'

"2. The following day, while I was engaged in other

work, this idea suddenly came to me, vague, indefinite and uncertain, something like this: Here is a *point*. Around a *point* there is a complete 'angular space' of 360 degrees (one whole angle). Must there not be something similar to this in the case of the closed figure? But this most hazy notion could not be further clarified at the time.

"Three days passed. Whatever I did, there was always present this same strong feeling, the feeling of something unfinished, of being directed toward something I could not grasp. I felt repeatedly that I could almost tell where the trouble lay, upon what it depended, in what direction the solution would develop, but it was all in a colloidal, indefinite state so that I could not formulate it concretely. Many times it seemed so clear that 'I need only write it down,' but when I attempted it, I could not, the ideas could not really be formulated. . . ."

In this description of his thought processes from Gestalt point of view Wertheimer ignores the stages of creative thought. For instance, he does not mention incubation, although it is revealed in the recurrence of the idea at intervals over a period of days. This is brought out in such descriptive phrases as: "After several hours it had developed to this stage," "The following day while I was engaged in other work, this idea suddenly came to me vague, indefinite, and uncertain, something like this:", "Three days passed. Whatever I did, there was always present this strong feeling, the feeling of something unfinished, of being directed toward something I could not grasp."

The vagueness and indefiniteness of the idea, which he mentions, is characteristic of incubation. Such statements, as the above show how the idea, which was incubated, recurred at intervals over a period of days. Wertheimer's period of incubation, which had extended over several days, was followed by the stage of illumination, in which the solution was reached, with the accompanying feeling of elation. This is seen in the statement, "Every side has two exterior right angles, one at each end. There can be as many sides, therefore as many such angles, as one wishes; but in every figure the σ's, the angles of rotation, must make a complete revolution. This was an 'intuition.' I was very happy at this moment. I had the feeling: 'Now I see through the matter.'"

The stages of creative thought are apparent in these protocols of Wertheimer, which show creative thinking in a complex mathematical problem. Yet Wertheimer overlooks the existence of these stages, which are obvious in this data he presents.

Summary

From the experimental data presented in this chapter we find the stage of incubation follows preparation in creative thinking, whether it be in the field of poetry, art, or science. The period of incubation is characterized by the recurrence of the chief idea, which is finally adopted as the solution to a problem or the subject of a work of art in the stage of illumination. This idea reappears spontaneously from time to time with modifications, as it recurs in different mental sets or configurations. Frequently the thinker has ceased making an effort to solve the problem and has turned his attention to other matters, as relaxation, recreation, physical exercise or other types of mental work. At the end of this stage, the idea which has been incubating is more clearly defined than it was at the beginning. Not only the chief idea, but also ideas, which are later discarded, may recur spontaneously from time to time with modifications during this period. The length of this stage may last from a few minutes or hours to months or even years. Sometimes in writing a short lyric poem or in sketching a picture the incubation stage may last a few minutes or days, while in making an invention, planning a scientific experiment, or writing a book it may extend over months or even years. The length of the period varies from person to person and also within the same individual from time to time, due to various factors, as the

nature of the original stimulating situation, the type of problem, personal habits, and manner of living. The stages of
preparation and incubation may overlap, and the spontaneous recurrence of the idea may be apparent, while the subject is still actively gathering information about the problem.

3

ILLUMINATION

The Third Stage

THE stage of illumination follows incubation. "Gradually an idea grows, annexing or using its neighbors, and becomes a mastering purpose which cannot be resisted. Finally it results in some creation." "Suddenly an illumination flashes upon us which we had perhaps longed for, perhaps not," according to Dimnet. Inspiration is brusk and instantaneous after slow maturation as described by Delacroix, while Hutchinson says that some sudden stimulus from this whole field of irrelevance coming into periods of slight mental preoccupation and after periods of rest, terminates the period of incubation and precipitates the period or moment of insight, the flood of ideas.

Sudden Appearance of Solution

Illumination is characterized by the suddenness with which the hunch or correct idea appears, whether in the field of science or art. Rossman found from his study of inventors that "after the problem has been dealt with objectively and is still unsolved, a new idea flashes upon the mind, a new pattern suddenly appears; a new relationship is seen." He quotes S. Olson as follows: The study of a problem "may take months or even years, taking it up and laying it down again a number of times—then when alone and at rest the substantial invention suddenly appears to my mind."

Rees shows how Durer received his inspiration at an unexpected moment. "In the night between Wednesday and Thursday after Whitsunday (30, 31 May, 1525) I saw this appearance in my sleep—how many great waters fell from heaven . . . so when I arose in the morning I painted it . . . as I saw it." Arnold Bennett received his insight in sudden flashes and often in the night: "I saw the whole play, in two acts, like a flash, and I described it." Cowell mentally rehearsed compositions which he heard at concerts. After a period of this self-training, he had "glorious sounds leap unexpectedly into his mind." Tschaikowsky[1] has said, "Generally, the germ of the work appears with lightning suddenness, quite unexpectedly. If this germ falls on fertile soil—that is to say, when the desire to work is felt—it takes root with incredible strength and rapidity, shoots up from the ground, displays branches, twigs, leaves, and finally blossoms. I cannot describe the process of creation otherwise than by this comparison. The greatest difficulty lies in the necessity that the germ should appear under favorable circumstances; then everything will proceed of its own accord."

Spontaneous Appearance of Solution

Another characteristic of illumination is that the "hunch" or correct idea appears spontaneously. Helmholtz emphasized this in an important speech given in 1896, when he said that after previous investigation of the problem "happy ideas came unexpectedly without effort like inspiration." Rignano likewise states, "If invention or inspiration is nothing more than a chance idea which at the moment of presenting itself is 'selected' from the rest by the corresponding affective tendency, it is natural it should present itself suddenly as if it had come of itself, without effort."

1 Rees (155)

The poet, J. G. Fletcher,[1] tells us how the chief idea for a poem may appear spontaneously. "Something which I have seen, heard, or experienced affects me very strongly. I brood upon it, largely unconscious, until suddenly, for no apparent reason, a line or group of lines form themselves in my brain, and in some way connected with the subject on which I have been thinking. . . . When I finally sit down to the actual task of composition, I generally . . . write the whole poem in a single draft. . . . This original draft may later be amplified or corrected, but never entirely re-written." Another poet, A. E. Housman, has similarly described the spontaneous and almost involuntary nature of such creation.

Galli obtained reports from various artists and writers concerning their general methods of working. At the time of inspiration the idea appears suddenly in the mind of the artist or inventor, without his seeking it. Often it comes as a brilliant flash, a new idea, without any evident reason. It does not appear through the power of attention. There is an impersonality about it, as Ribot has pointed out, which appears like a power superior to the conscious individual.

With music Mozart[2] has said that the composition "does not come to me successively, with its various parts worked out in detail, as they will be later on, but it is in its entirety that my imagination lets me hear it." This spontaneity is reflected in John Philip Sousa's[3] remark, "Any composer who is gloriously conscious that he is a composer must believe that he receives his inspiration from a source higher than himself." Bahle, who sent poems to thirty composers, requesting that they compose music about one of them, used the questionnaire method and obtained reports of how they did it. One composer said that the inspiration was best compared to the "appearance of a spirit" in an occult seance after everything was prepared. Another stated that "he always had the feeling that the idea is outside of time and space,

---

[1] Portnoy (149)   [2] Hadamard (58)   [3] Rees (155)

that it was generated in the background of his feelings and thoughts, and that it was not native."

Similarly Harding writes, "Whichever form the inspiration takes it comes unsought as a gift without any kind of effort at the time on the part of the recipient. . . . An idea or an impression which comes into the mind without effort is an inspiration irrespective of its triviality or value." It usually has a sense of value with it. "The recipient feels himself to be possessed by some power whilst he is nothing but its mouthpiece or instrument. . . . The state of inspiration is not directly under the control of the will. . . . The decisive idea has the way of appearing when the mind is passive and even contemplating nothing in particular." Along this line, Platt and Baker have presented a quotation from a chemist, who said that a scientific hunch "invariably comes at night after retiring for sleep, and the insight has been entirely effortless." Hutchinson aptly points out, "If one had the least vestige of superstition, it is easy to see how he might suppose himself to be merely the incarnation, merely the mouthpiece, merely the medium of higher forces. It is the impersonality and automatic production of such moments of inspiration that has led to endless theories of extrapersonal revelation."

Feeling of Confidence

Another characteristic of illumination is the feeling of certainty and confidence which accompanies the appearance of the hunch or solution. Bahle points out that the characteristics of the "sudden idea" are its fitness for the problem at hand, its capacity for expansion, and its vitality, freshness, and originality. Wallas terms it the "happy idea." Inspiration has been defined as "an instantaneous grasping of the solution of a problem, or of a proper method of procedure, or of the plan of a work of art, without the usual intermediate steps of association and reasoning."

Platt and Baker, who obtained reports from chemists on

methods of work, describe a scientific hunch as "a unifying or clarifying idea which springs into consciousness suddenly as a solution to a problem in which we are intensely interested. In typical cases it follows a long study, but comes into consciousness at a time when we are not working on the problem. A hunch springs from a wide knowledge of facts, but is essentially a leap of the imagination, in that it goes beyond a mere necessary conclusion which any reasonable man must draw from the data at hand."

The feeling of confidence and certainty, which accompanies the appearance of the solution, is evident in the following account by the mathematician, Poincare: "Then I turned my attention to the study of some arithmetical questions apparently without much success and without a suspicion of any connection with my preceding researches. Disgusted with my failure, I went to spend a few days at the seaside, and thought of something else. One morning, walking on the bluff, the idea came to me, with just the same characteristics of brevity, suddenness and immediate certainty, that the arithmetic transformations of indeterminate ternary quadratic forms were identical with those of non-Euclidean geometry."

Feeling of Pleasure or Elation

An emotional reaction generally accompanies this stage, although not always. This may range in intensity from pleasant contentment to intense joy or elation. Such emotional reaction appears in the personal experience of the poet, A. E. Housman: "I would go out for a walk of two or three hours. As I went along, thinking of nothing in particular . . . there would flow into my mind, with sudden and unaccountable emotion, sometimes a line or two of verse, sometimes a whole stanza at once."

Snyder describes the writing of hypnotic poems, as he terms them, and stresses the psychological effect of rhythm in leading to a state of trance and in intensifying emotional

susceptibility. The poet puts himself in a trance by repeating the first lines of the poem to himself in autohypnosis. "As
he repeats over and over what he has composed and dwells
with increased concentration on a single phase of life, he
gradually experiences the trance in which, for the time being,
nothing else is of any importance or indeed enters into his
consciousness." In a light state of trance his full artistic
powers are liberated. Portnoy points out that the illumination stage finds "the artist in his glory. Ideas flow, the eye
sees, the ear hears, the artist is keenly alive again. He works
with abundant energy until exhausted." The composer often
works in such a feverish state that the hand cannot keep up
with the thought, according to the reports which Galli obtained from various artists and writers.

Length of Stage

The stage of illumination is of brief duration as Ribot
points out when he writes that this phase "is only an instant,
but essential—the moment of discovery." With it the work
is virtually ended. The flowering occurs "when this latent
work is complete" in the phase of incubation and "the idea
suddenly bursts forth." Prescott notes the emergence of the
thought into the conscious mind at an "inspired moment."
Insight "lasts for a moment or at most a few hours, isolating
the thinker from his normal world," according to Hutchinson. Likewise Harding stresses the evanescence of inspira-
tional ideas and impressions which are sharp and clear at the
time, yet quickly forgotten if not recorded. "Inspiration
does not continue long."

This brief duration is brought out in the quotations
from chemists studied by Platt and Baker: "I had worked
on the problem until my mind and body were completely
fatigued. I decided to abandon work and all thought relative thereto and then, on the following day, when occupied
in work of an entirely different type, an idea came to my
mind as suddenly as a flash of lightning and it was the solu-

tion." "We had worked on it quite intensively for several months, and after that only occasionally. One day while sitting at my desk doing nothing and thinking about other matters, a thought flashed through my mind." It was the solution.

The illumination period is frequently a matter of moments, although it may last hours. It is to be contrasted with the stages of preparation and incubation, which may last days, months, or even years. Hartmann describes illumination as "the brief but critical period when all the brain work earlier done on a problem crystallizes in a flash of extraordinarily rapid organization. The melody for which one has been searching now begins to take form, or, in another area of creativity, the ideas literally come faster than one can write them down. This is the moment—really, many moments, sometimes hours—of 'inspiration' for which the individual has longed."

Relation to Insight in Simpler Problems

Illumination is a special case of insight, which has been studied in both animals and people by a number of investigators, especially of the Gestalt school. Illumination is the term applied to insight, which occurs when a problem is sufficiently difficult in relation to the ability of the subject so that the four stages of creative thought are present.

Ogden employs insight as the "term for noting an intelligent behavior in which the 'why' is registered by an appropriate discrimination of desire, means, and end; that is to say, appropriate in the only way in which anything is 'realistically' or 'objectively' appropriate." It "implies that behavior is intrinsically meaningful."

Experiments on animals have provided much of the data for descriptions and definitions of insight. Kohler concludes, "The insightful performance is an integrated whole conforming to the configuration or structure of the situation. Such a solution may occur at the first contact with the problem or after other attempts, lacking insight, have been made. The suddenness with which the solution often emerges indicates insight, and another index is found in the transfer of the solution to a somewhat modified problem." From work with apes Yerkes describes the hesitant behavior and more or less adequate modes of response followed by the appearance of a critical point at which the organism suddenly, directly, and definitely performs the required adaptive act.

After Alpert had studied forty-four nursery-school children he wrote, "The arousal of insight and its consummation in a practical solution are favored by emotional, temperamental, and mental factors—those which in effect constituted the total personality. This is true in a far lesser degree of apes, probably because of their lower level development."

Maier presented problems to fifty-two adults and found that mere experience or even selection of pertinent experiences was not enough to solve the problems. It was necessary to have the integration of the parts in terms of the goal and the experiencing of new relations. Storring gave his subjects two premises from which a conclusion was to be drawn and found there was an "aha-experience," a moment of insight, in which the two premises shot together into a unitary pattern. Wheeler has pointed out that "periods of initial delay prior to the execution of a new performance, that is hesitating while studying a novel situation, that is presumably a symptom that the configuration is forming."

An investigation of insight in simple and more complex situations was carried out by Durkin, who requested her subjects to construct six two-dimension puzzles. Five of them consisted of several pieces to be put into square or Maltese crosses, while the more difficult sixth was a large cross consisting of all of the pieces of the five simple puzzles. Sudden reorganization appeared almost entirely with the most difficult one, which was beyond the person's "apprehension span."

"It has often been pointed out that such restructurations

play an important role in thinking, in problem solving," according to Duncker. "The decisive points in thought-processes, the moments of sudden comprehension, of the 'Aha!' of the new, are always at the same time moments in which such a sudden restructuring of the thought-material takes place, in which something 'tips over.' " It is "this restructuration, more precisely: this transformation of function within a system, which causes more or less difficulty for thinking, as one individual or another tries to find a mathematical proof.

"If a situation is introduced in a certain perceptual structuration, and if this structure is still 'real' or 'alive,' thinking achieves a contrary structuration only against the resistance of the former structure. The degree of this difficulty varies among individuals." Duncker finds that insight is both gradual and graduated. It is gradual, according to Duncker, in the sense that the solution of a complex problem proceeds by steps, which are themselves insightful. It is graduated in the sense that one may see more or less deeply into a situation. The lower degree is present when a person knows a rule and realizes the given situation is one where the rule is applicable. In the higher degree, the person comprehends the reason for the rule. Duncker obtained protocols from subjects who solved a scientific problem.

Claparede gave people the task of finding the subject of comic drawings or telling the story in a series of pictures. They were instructed, "Think, reflect aloud; say all that passes within your mind during the time you work to find the solution of the problem." Thinking was found to take a zigzag course. Claparede observed "the sudden appearance of an idea or hypothesis." The whole situation was clarified immediately. "In the light of this new element the appearance of the former elements is changed."

Evidence of insight was studied in the responses of thirty-two high school students to nine geometric originals and fourteen underlying theorems. Henry writes, "Insight is

present in certain instances in solving geometric originals.
. . . However, it would not be correct to characterize the
typical successful behavior as the operation of insight," in
this experiment.

Thus, we find insight is present in various degrees in different types of problems, and appears at times in the reactions of the great apes and children. Let us reserve the term
"illumination" for the type of insight which appears, when
the problem is sufficiently difficult in relation to the ability
of the subject, so as to produce creative thinking. Illumination is typically preceded by the stages of preparation and
incubation, which may be lacking in simpler problems.

Patrick's experiments show that illumination follows
preparation and incubation in poetic, artistic, and scientific
thinking. This is evident with the poets, artists, and average
persons doing poetic and artistic thinking, as well as with
those engaging in scientific thinking. It is characteristic of
both the skilled and unskilled.

Insight occurs in situations ranging from the simple perceptual problem, in which the relation of the significant factors is ascertained almost immediately, through the various
simple and more complex problems, and it also occurs in
creative thought. In the perceptual problem the correct response is recognized almost at once as the correct solution to
the problem. In more difficult problems the relationship of
the significant factors is not apprehended until after reasoning of a simple or more complex nature has occurred. In
simple reasoning situations, after the subject has thought of
some alternatives, the first time the correct response occurs
it is recognized as the correct solution to the problem, and
thus the solution is reached within the first attempts made
during the stage of preparation. Such a situation is, for example, the solving of a simple mechanical puzzle. Here we frequently find only the stage of preparation terminated by the
correct response, which is recognized as the solution the
first time it occurs. In more complex problems of creative

thought, incubation follows preparation although it may overlap with the first stage. An idea recurs from time to time and is modified each time it appears, until at last it is recognized in the stage of illumination or insight as the correct solution. The preparation and incubation stages may last weeks, months, or even years.

Thus we find insight appearing in various problem situations, ranging from those so simple that they are solved almost immediately, through those of increasing complexity to the very complicated problems of creative thought.

Insight typically occurs in the response of an organism to a situation which is novel to it. If the situation is very familiar to the subject, habit rather than insight will provide the solution. A primary condition for the appearance of insight, then, is that it must have the aspect of novelty for the organism at the time the response is made. Either the situation must be novel for the subject, or, if the situation is somewhat familiar, the subject must have forgotten what he did before, so that he reacts as if he were in a novel situation.

Let us reserve the term "illumination" to apply to insight which occurs in the complicated problems which induce creative thinking. Let us apply the term illumination to insight, which has been preceded by the stages of preparation and incubation, and which are often lacking in very simple problems, where insight may occur almost immediately. Illumination, then, is the third stage of creative thought, which follows preparation and incubation. It is more often accompanied by an emotional reaction of intense pleasure or elation, than is true of insight in simpler problems.

Summary

Illumination is the third stage of creative thought, during which the idea which has been incubating assumes definite form. In composing a poem or painting a picture it is typically the period when the lines are first formulated or the outline of the picture is first sketched. In solving a scientific problem it is the period when the solution is first conceived. In making an invention it is the stage when the model is first designed. In legal work it is the period when a new interpretation is first conceived. In composing music it is when the theme is first written. The idea appears suddenly. It comes spontaneously, with a feeling of certainty. It is typically accompanied by an emotional reaction of pleasure, even joy or elation. This stage is generally of short duration. While insight may occur in all kinds of problems, even the most simple, illumination is applied to the insight which appears in the complicated problems of creative thinking, where it has been preceded by the stages of preparation and incubation.

4

VERIFICATION OR REVISION

The Fourth Stage

VERIFICATION or revision is the final stage in the creative process. Wallas, after describing the stages of Preparation, Incubation, and Illumination writes, "And I shall add a fourth stage of Verification." Galli asserts that the work of art is not complete at the time of inspiration, but there must be revision and criticism. Claparede likewise says that the final operation in the intellectual act consists of verification.

Mozart[1] has described his thinking by stating that after his imagination lets him hear how a composition will sound in its entirety in the stage of illumination, the various parts are worked out in detail in the final stage. "The main function of inspiration in artistic work is, therefore, to provide the nucleus from which the work develops," according to Harding. This is what Luzzatto refers to when he says the final moment is that of execution. Duncker makes reference to verification and revision when he asserts that a final stage of the reasoning process is the positive elaboration of penetration and the realization or execution of the functional value. The final or specific solution is the application of a functional solution to the available data of the situation (supplemented by one's store of personal experiences). Simi-

1 Hadamard (58)

41

larly Ogden points out that psychological judgment, which appears in the final stage of reasoning, "signifies the refinement of a configuration, with respect both to its contour and its inner articulation, the direction of refinement being determined by the law of precision."

Amount of Work or Effort

The revision may be slight or involve much effort. Rees says, "Elaboration is personal for the artist, for the means which he uses he must discover. . . . The way in which the artist elaborates is important to him. Artists have less to say about this phase of the creative process than about any other. It is almost too close for them to be able to divulge it." She quotes Robert Schumann and tells "how he carefully thinks through his work, and at the same time points out the variation which exists among the artists in their ways of thinking: 'But I certainly feel that theoretical studies have had a good influence upon me. Formerly I wrote down everything on the impulse of the moment, but now I follow the course of my ideas more, and sometimes stop short and look around to see where I am.' "

The effort involved in elaboration and revision is revealed by Prescott when he writes, "There is first the sudden inspiration, then the laborious composition. . . . The pictures presented by the poetic imagination in its sudden vision must often be worked over and connected by ordinary thought to take their place in the poem."

There is need to verify the idea obtained by "inspiration," according to Poincare. When a sudden illumination comes in mathematical thinking, it must stand the test of verification. "All that we can hope from these inspirations, which are the fruits of unconscious work, is to obtain points of departure for such calculations. The calculations themselves must be made in the second period of conscious work which follows the inspiration. The rules of the calculations are strict and complicated; they demand discipline, attention, will, and consequently consciousness."

Revision by Standards of Art or Science

In verification and revision the idea, which has been obtained in illumination, is made to conform to the standards of art or science by special disciplines and techniques. In this stage of mathematical thinking, according to Wallas, both the validity of the idea is tested, and the idea itself reduced to exact form. Verification "closely resembles the first stage of preparation." It is usually fully conscious. Men have worked out much the same series of mathematical and logical rules for controlling verification by conscious effort as those used in the control of preparation. This testing of the idea is indicated by Collins[2] when he writes, "After the mental image is formed I go into the shop."

In the final stage or that of verification, elaboration or evaluation, the exaggerations of the period of insight are checked against external realities, as Hutchinson points out. "Without this insight, not much of social value would be released." The period of verification or elaboration is characterized by systematic, "exacting work and largely uninspired." "The problem of objectification presents itself as an almost unexpected responsibility, demanding a shift in mental attitude toward the critical side." There is the "application of all rules of procedure and special techniques, concern over materials, media, and paraphernalia of actual production . . . to hammer the ideational contribution of insight into some form of objective or tangible reality. . . . All too often because of the high cost in mental effort, endeavor stops short of this final realization." The future of the project remains uncertain. The elaboration process has subtleties, which in one sense make it psychologically almost as complex as the period of insight. Hutchinson describes characteristics of elaboration, as the nature of the critical at-

2 Rossman (162)

titude, the visitation of secondary insights, the limited capacity of the creator as critic, the dominance of negative standards of criticism over positive, the effect of certain aids to criticism upon the mental process, constantly shifting orientation of interest between criticism and creation, the reaction to the finished work. The critical attitude "owes its power to the perception of contrasts between work in the process of development and the standards, both implicit and explicit, which it must satisfy. . . . In the struggle to materialize the project, the grounds for the rejection of materials are naturally more explicit than the grounds for acceptance, because the only things upon which the critical faculty can with assurance fasten are the elements common to the new insight and what was known and explicit concerning it prior to its appearance. . . . When elaboration entails deletion of parts of a work already completed, the destruction requires almost as great a force of mind, or great expenditure of psychic energy as the act of creation." "The history of both art and science is largely the history of man's personal endurance, his acceptance of labor as the price of success. . . . Elaboration is for the mature only; it is for the rigorous, the exacting, the profound."

Length of Stage

The length of the period of revision or verification may last only a short time or extend into months or years. The duration of this stage varies according to the nature and difficulty of the problem or work of art, and according to other factors. Ribot says, "How false is the theory that holds that there is always a sudden stroke of inspiration, followed by a period of rapid or slow execution. On the contrary, observation reveals many processes that apparently differ less in the content of invention than according to individual temperament." Ribot outlines two processes of creative thought: the complete process, in which the final phase is verification or application; the abridged process, in which the final phase is the constructive and developing period. The two processes differ superficially rather than essentially. In both processes the third phase may be long or short because the main work is done. "Elaboration may be years of grinding work; the perspiration that is nine-tenths genius," according to Hutchinson.

Verification or revision was easily identified in the data which Patrick obtained on scientific, artistic and poetic thinking.

The Four Stages May Overlap

The four stages, which we have discussed in the preceding chapters, may overlap. Incubation may appear during preparation and revision may begin in the illumination stage.

Hutchinson mentions this fact when he says, "The act of critical elaboration may begin immediately after the appearance of insight, or form a period co-existent with it." Or it may wait a while after the first draft. "In fact, one of the most effective agents in encouraging the swing in mental attitude away from the distinctly creative toward the critical is time." It must be sufficient for the thinker to regain his objective reference. "The critical attitude is as essentially unstable, as difficult to maintain as the creative. . . . Minor or secondary insights come so frequently and with such force that it is sometimes better to consider the period of elaboration as co-extensive with, if not identical to, the original period of insight. . . . The alterations exist because the creative mind is dynamic, because the polarity creation-criticism is dependent upon the subject-object, self-outer world relation, in which the mind by its very structure—as the psychoanalysts have often pointed out—is inevitably bound to oscillate . . . continual, although not regular, alteration is the rule so long as the creative impulse does not atrophy."

It is not uncommon for incubation to overlap with preparation. An idea, which leads to the solution, may begin to recur from time to time, while the thinker is still collecting information about the problem. Although illumination is typically of short duration, yet sometimes revision starts while the artist or scientist is formulating the main outline for his work of art or the solution to his problem.

Any description of creative thought must take cognizance of the fact that in a complex problem different phases of the subject might develop differently. For instance, in a scientific experiment it might be necessary to develop several different methods of testing different aspects of the problem. Thus the thinker might have reached the illumination stage and know the procedure for testing one aspect of the problem, while still floundering around in the preparation stage on another aspect of the problem. And he still might be incubating a third aspect of the problem, while doing different tasks. Or in the artistic field, in the case of a person writing a long epic poem, the poet might have conceived of the general scheme of the poem during the stages of preparation, incubation, and illumination. The writing of one section of it, which may be a little poem inside the larger one, might be only at the preparation stage, while another section may have been developed to the final stage of revision.

In a complex problem, as typical of creative thought, various stages may appear in different aspects of the same problem, at the same time. If the problem is a very difficult one this phenomenon is apt to occur. The complex problem may of itself be composed of lesser problems, each of which are sufficiently difficult to induce creative thinking.

Summary

The final stage of creative thought is verification or revision. The essential idea, or outline, which appeared in the illumination stage, is revised or verified. In the writing of a poem the author examines the lines, which he wrote during the stage of illumination, to add some details and eliminate others. In the solving of a scientific problem, the scientist may employ statistical techniques or laboratory equipment to verify the idea which he obtained in illumination. The artist adds and eliminates colors and lines to the picture which he has sketched, while the musician plays his composition on the appropriate musical instrument to see what notes and chords should be changed. The idea obtained in illumination is made to conform to the standards of art or science by special disciplines or techniques. The revision may be slight or involve much effort. The duration of this stage may vary from a few minutes to months or years, depending on the nature and difficulty of the problem. The four stages may overlap, as incubation may appear during preparation and revision may begin during the illumination stage.

5

EXPLANATIONS OF INCUBATION AND CREATIVE THOUGHT

The Subconscious Mind

"THE part played by this unconscious work in mathematical discovery seems to me indisputable, and we shall find traces of it in other cases where it is less evident," writes Poincare. . . . "The unconscious ego, as it is called, the subliminal ego, plays a most important part in mathematical discovery. It has been said that the subliminal ego is automatic, but that is not true. It is in no way inferior to the conscious ego. . . . It is capable of discernment, it has tact, and lightness of touch; it can select, and it can divine. . . . Combinations which present themselves to mind in a sort of sudden illumination, after an unconscious working somewhat prolonged, are generally useful and fertile combinations." Poincare says that in mathematical problems "it never happens that the subconscious mind supplies ready-made the result of a lengthy calculation in which we have only to apply fixed rules. It might be supposed that the subliminal ego "was peculiarly fitted for this kind of work. . . . All that we can hope from these inspirations, which are the fruits of unconscious work, is to obtain points of departure for such calculations. The calculations themselves must be made in the second period of conscious work which follows the inspiration. The rules of these calculations are strict and complicated; they demand discipline, attention, will, and consequently consciousness. In the subliminal ego, on the contrary, there reigns what I would call liberty, if one could give this name to the mere absence of discipline and to the disorder born of chance. Only, this very disorder permits of unexpected couplings."

Similarly Jastrow says, "There exists in all intellectual endeavor a period of incubation, a process in great part subconscious, a slow concealed maturing through absorption of a suitable problem. Schopenhauer calls it 'unconscious rumination.' . . . The thesis implied by such terms has two aspects: first, that the process of assimilation may take place with suppressed consciousness; second, that the larger part of the influences that in the end determine our mental growth, may be effective without direct exposure to the searching light of conscious life." "Sensory experience followed by a period of gestation and then the act of artistic creation seems to be the inevitable cycle whether we consider music, poetry, the drama, or the novel," according to Portnoy. "Impressions and memories received through the senses undergo a period of incubation or unconscious elaboration."

The thinker is unaware of the processes of the unconscious mind. "It functions as an entity to determine present behavior not by mere additive co-operation with other factors, but by providing basic regulative framework within which these other factors, as present stimuli, special habits, or trial and error may function. It may function autonomously without the mediation of conscious states upon the situation," according to Bartlett. Often the idea comes as a brilliant flash, without any evident reason, from an atmosphere more or less subconscious, in Galli's opinion.

Rapaport writes, "When an unconscious idea arises to consciousness, the ego suspends its 'censoring' function momentarily, only to resume it again."

The influence of previous conscious experience on the

activity of the subconscious is brought out by Downey, who asserts, "Inspiration may be a flash-up from the unconscious, but it is no chance explosion occurring indifferently." Likewise Gesell says that the "so-called unconscious cerebration can take place only as a result of purposeful endeavor," and Ribot points out that there is "sudden eruption into consciousness, but one presupposing a latent, frequently long, labor." "In inspiration, then, there is first a long preparation of the mind, then a period of incubation, and finally an emergence of the thought into the conscious mind at an 'inspired moment.' The conscious mind is perhaps often vaguely and uneasily aware of the process of incubation," according to Prescott. Similarly Wallas speaks of unconscious incubation. Hadamard states that in the period of incubation before the illumination phase more or less unconscious processes play a significant part. Likewise, Humphrey says that in "all probability some form of working that is unconscious must be postulated to explain these cases."

In describing creative thought the importance of unconscious desires has been stressed. Revesz states that conscious work and spontaneous, unconscious inspiration operate together. Delacroix says that the aesthetic creation is an imaginary satisfaction of unconscious desires in which the projection replaces the impossible satisfaction. Ungratified wishes in the conscious mind take up their abode in the subconscious mind where they initiate the thinking process, according to Rossman. The will to solve a problem or create a work of art is a big factor in creative thought. "The earnest wish to get at the whole thing should be the chief thing acting on our subconscious," writes Dimnet.

Lowes describes how Coleridge produced his great poems: "One after another vivid bits from what he had read dropped into that deep well. And there, below the level of conscious mental processes they set up their obscure and powerful reactions. Up above, on the stream of consciousness (which is all that we commonly take into account) they had floated separate and remote. . . . Facts which sank at intervals out of conscious recollection drew together beneath the surface. . . . And when the flash of inspiration at last came . . . that leap of association which, like the angel in the Gospel, stirred to momentary potency the waters of the pool —it was neither fish, nor animalcula, nor snakelike things, nor veritable watersnakes, but these radiant creatures of the subliminal abyss that sported on the face of a sea lit by a moon which had risen from the same abyss." "These larger factors of the creative process—the storing of the Well, the Vision, and the concurrent operation of the Will—are not the monopoly of poetry. Through their conjunction the imagination in the field of science, for example, is slowly drawing the immense confusion of phenomena within the unfolding conception of an ordered universe. And its operations are essentially the same."

A similar explanation is given by Feibleman who writes, "The bulk of the artistic imagination takes place in the unconscious or psyche of the individual. . . . The psychological life of the human individual is comparable to the iceberg which is always more than three-quarters submerged. The consciousness floats like a film upon the surface of the unconscious and hardly more than represents the multitudinous activities of the whole psyche. . . . The relation between the conscious and unconscious parts of the psychological realm . . . is still unknown. So far as the psychology of art is concerned, however, what we can claim to know is that the artistic process involves them both."

Effect of Rest and Different Mental Sets

The explanation of creative thought and incubation in terms of the subconscious mind constitutes only one of several theories which have been offered. For instance, Rignano asserts that normal reasoning is produced almost entirely in the conscious state and that unconscious elaboration does not take place at all, since the supposed unconscious elaboration is not the least fatiguing. "Each psychical state is, in itself, neither conscious, nor unconscious, but becomes one or the other only in relation to some other psychical state serving as a point of reference." If invention or inspiration is nothing more than a chance idea which "at the moment of presenting itself is 'selected' from the rest by the corresponding affective tendency it is natural it should present itself suddenly, as if it had come of itself, without effort—that it should seem to rise up from the depths of the unconscious." He adds that the inspiration mentioned by Poincare is not in the unconscious "but everything took place openly, that is to say in the full presence of consciousness, and that this character of 'sudden illumination,' of 'brevity, suddenness, and certainty,' on which he lays so much emphasis, is here due solely to the fact of a fortuitous combination of ideas, entering into activity at this moment." It is hard to regard reasoning as "operative in the unconscious state while the conscious activity of the individual is occupied with other things, and this because of the considerable duration, amplitude, and intensity of the subconscious affectivity that such an unconscious reasoning would presuppose. Much less is this possible for the sort of reasoning which is supposed to constitute the long and difficult elaboration leading to the inspiration." Rignano considers "normal reasoning is produced almost exclusively in the conscious state, and that, consequently, the share of the unconscious in reasoning itself and in inspiration is almost entirely nil."

Harding likewise discredits the importance of the unconscious in the following statements, "We do not believe that the subconscious mind provides the solution by itself. In the first place the subconscious mind can only provide the solution if the necessary ideas are already stored in the mind; and secondarily, it is far from likely that a problem in an important piece of scientific work could be set aside and entirely forgotten. . . . The problem is not forgotten but merely set aside." It is not relegated to the depths of the sub-conscious mind.

Helmholtz has shown that the modifications during the period of incubation were due to the overcoming of fatigue and the handling of the material better. Happy ideas "have never come to me when my mind was fatigued, or when I was at my working table. . . . They came particularly readily during the slow ascent of wooded hills on a sunny day."

In a similar manner Woodworth shows it is not necessary to use the unconscious as an explanation. "The word 'incubation' rather implies the theory of unconscious work on a problem during a period of attention to other matters, but we can strip off this implication and use it simply to denote the fact—so far as it is a fact—that a period of inattention to a problem intervenes after preparation and before illumination. . . . Apart from the theory of unconscious work—unconscious cerebration, it has also been called—the facts observed by Poincare in his thinking are essentially the same as those reported by Helmholtz. After the necessary preliminary period of intensive work in becoming familiar with the problem, there must be a period of rest, or perhaps of unconscious work, before a new idea can be expected. This new idea needs to be verified and elaborated before the discovery can be called complete. But what is really new about the discovery emerges suddenly after preparation and a period of inattention to the problem." "The obvious theory—unconscious work, whether conceived as mental or as cerebral—should be left as a residual hypothesis for adoption only if other, more testable hypotheses break down. . . . Since the problem does consciously recur from time to time during the period of incubation, though without effortful work done upon it, partial solutions may be obtained. . . . If it is true that the illumination comes in a period, short or long, of intense concentration on the problem, the assumption of previous unconscious work is gratuitous.

"The freshness or lack of brain fatigue which seems to be

necessary for illumination may furnish a sufficient explanation.

"The parallel but simpler case of the recall of a name, after futile attempts followed by dropping the matter, suggests that an essential factor in illumination is the absence of interferences which block progress during the preliminary stage. When, as must often happen, the thinker makes a false start, he slides insensibly into a groove and may not be able to escape at the moment. He falls into certain assumptions which restrict his sector of exploratory activity, just as in other cases of problem solving, and as long as he continues actively at work in this sector he does not escape from these assumptions, as he often does on coming back to the problem after giving it a rest. Several of the inventors noted a fact which favors this interpretation: the happy idea, when it came, amazed them by its simplicity. They had assumed a more complicated solution to be necessary. According to this line of evidence, incubation consists in getting rid of false leads and hampering assumptions so as to approach the problem with an 'open mind.' "

In their discussion of incubation Shaffer, Gilmer and Schoen point out "the part played by sleep, idleness, and change of occupation. After continuous work on a problem many inhibitions and interferences are set up. Relaxation allows these to die out, and permits a fresh approach to be made. When an inspiration comes in the midst of conversation or during other unrelated work, it is probable that some unnoticed stimulus has provoked a return to the original problem, which is solved immediately because of the absence of the old conflicts and confusions."

Meinicke indicates the importance of difference of mental set at the time of discovery in the report of an engineer, who invented a machine to portion dough in a bakery. He had worked on the problem without success for a long time, and became tired and laid the problem aside. He was accustomed to take a walk along the river bank. There was a paddle steamboat, which he had been accustomed to see, but on a particular day there was also a new dredge. As he returned home past a bakery shop, he received the successful idea for an invention, which combined the principles of the dredge and the revolving paddle of the steamboat.

Ruger studied changes in mental set in relation to discovery. In discussing the reactions of subjects in the solution of mechanical puzzles he says, "The general assumptions which the subjects made concerning the nature of the special problem in hand were often set up accidentally and became thoroughly entrenched without being subjected to criticism. . . . The assumptions thus uncritically set up in some cases limited the movements made by the subject to a certain portion of the puzzle, and, consequently, in some instances, rendered the solution impossible. . . . These fixed assumptions, which had an inertia about them, were broken up in several ways. . . . In some cases the puzzle was solved almost immediately on coming back to it later in the day. The particular set of consciousness had been broken up by this change and new points of view were now possible. There were a number of rather striking cases of a similar sort on first awakening in the morning." According to Thorndike, we should "avoid the common mistake of supposing that creations, in the brain or elsewhere, cannot be as truly determined as the formation of water by the union of hydrogen and oxygen."

Guetzkow writes, "The delineation of two processes in the operation of set (susceptibility to set and the ability to surmount set) was confirmed. . . . Set was more obvious and easily noticeable in the higher mental processes than in those tasks more closely related to sensory or motor functions."

Gestalt Interpretation

Explanations of reasoning and productive thinking in Gestalt terms have been offered by other investigators. Wheeler writes, "A man behaves only when under tension, and behavior is a process of resolving the tension. The resolving, in turn, is effected by reaching the goal. The act is terminated because reaching the goal completes, relatively at least, the establishing of an equilibrium between stresses within the organism. But note that it is behavior—doing something with reference to an environmental objective—that brings about the equilibrium. The resolution of tension within the organism is synonymous with an approach to the goal." Unified response implies "that an act has begun as the result of tension; that the movements involved are integrated toward an end or goal, established before the movement commenced; that the differentials in stress within the muscles and nerves are always so aligned or balanced that the movements occur in the line of least action." "It is fast becoming evident that all behavior is configurational: Learning, memory, emotion, thinking, perception and sensory processes included; and recently it has been discovered that a similar set of laws holds for the physiological activities of the nervous system."

Likewise, Hartmann says, "A need is basic to all learning. A need corresponds to a state of tension in the system. The tension itself seems to be a consequence of the physical, mental, or social 'field' in which the learner is embedded. This is the motivating power that keeps the learner active in the pursuit of his objectives until his tension is reduced or removed by the altered organization of his field."

Kohler and Koffka write from a similar point of view. Kohler says, "It becomes evident here that, in contrast to the indifferent mosaic of sensations assumed in older theory, this order of the field shows a strong 'predilection' for certain general kinds of organization as against others, exactly as the formation of molecules and the working of surface forces in physics operates in certain definite directions." Koffka asserts that "a stimulus upsets an equilibrium on the receptive side of the system; this upset equilibrium results in a movement which tends to bring the system to a new equilibrium and consequently the reaction must vary with the way in which the equilibrium was disturbed, that is with the receptor process, with the phenomenal situation."

The Gestalt interpretation is presented by Eindhoven and Vinacke. They state that "creativity is a dynamic whole." They observed 13 artists and 14 non-artists, who made illustrations for a poem.

Bloom and Broder studied the role of thought organization into foreground-background relationships by having students "think aloud," as they solved problems.

A description of thinking from the Gestalt point of view is presented by Duncker. "Between the moment the organism is confronted with the problem and the moment the final solution is achieved there occur, as a rule, a number of intermediate steps leading, in a hierarchical fashion, from general to more specific features of the sought-after solution." "Problem solving behavior . . . consists of a reduction of a general range or means-end-readiness to a more specific functional solution and then to still more specific solutions or specific hypotheses until the solution is achieved." He further writes, "The solution-process continues until 'the gap is closed,' 'the organization is complete,' 'the disturbance is removed,' 'equilibrium or release of tension is attained,' and this is undoubtedly relevant from the dynamical or, more correctly, the energy point of view. But of what kinds of events this 'tendency toward equilibrium' or toward 'pragnanz' can make use, this is the problem which must now be investigated in the light of gestalt psychology. . . . We observed that solution which involves a re-centering, a change of aspect, of the given material can be facilitated if the new aspect is somehow brought into prominence, and thereby made more accessible to an analysis of premises. . . . A solution always arises 'out of demands made by what is required on what is given.' Consequently, a solution, specifically a helpful restructuration of material, may be facilitated or hindered from two sides: not only by suitable variation of what is given ('from below') but also by suitable variation of the demand ('from above'). . . .

"We can formulate the general proposition that a suggestion is the sooner understood or assimilated, the closer it approaches the genealogical line already under development, and, within this line, the nearer it is to the problem-phase then in operation: in short, the more completely it is already anticipated. . . . Such a transition to phases in another line takes place typically when some tentative solution does not satisfy, or when one makes no further progress in a given direction. Another solution, more or less clearly defined, is then looked for. . . . It will be realized that, in the transition to phases in another line, the thought-process may range more or less widely. Every such transition involves a return to an earlier phase of the problem; an earlier task is set anew; a new branching off from an old point in the family tree occurs. Sometimes S returns to the original setting of the problem, sometimes just to the immediately preceding phase."

In a similar manner Wertheimer writes, "When one grasps a problem situation, its structural features and requirements set up certain strains, stresses, tensions in the thinker. What happens in real thinking is that these strains and stresses are followed up, yield vectors in the direction of improvement of the situation, and change it accordingly. S2 is a state of affairs that is held together by inner forces as a good structure in which there is harmony in the mutual requirements, and in which the parts are determined by the structure of the whole, as the whole is by the parts.

"The process does not involve the given parts and their transformations. It works in conjunction with material that is structurally relevant, but is selected from past experience, from previous knowledge and orientation.

"In all this, such movements, steps, are strongly preferred as change the state of affairs in S1 along a structurally consistent line into S2.

"If this is basically the nature of the process, i.e., if the steps are structurally determined, then various questions arise, for instance, why often the process does not proceed more directly, why there are states in which no progress is made, why the development may come to a dead stop and often remain blocked for some time—how deviations, mistakes originate. I have mentioned some of the reasons. I may repeat that a first inadequate view of the situation will often prevent the subject from grasping the real structure of the gap and the nature of the requirements that would enable him to close it adequately. Often the subject is lacking in breadth of view. Even when he has it at the beginning, he may lose it in the process because he is busy with details or falls into a piecemeal attitude. Under these circumstances closure may tend to occur in regions that are too narrow. On the other hand, of course, a subject's view may be over-extended."

Creative Thought and Learning

From this consideration of different descriptions of creative and productive thinking let us try to get a better understanding of the nature of the process. A problem situation induces an unfulfilled want in the organism which is accompanied by a disturbance of equilibrium in the nervous system and which is registered in consciousness by the awareness of the problem. The solution is the response with its accompanying neural correlate which terminates the want and restores the equilibrium in the nervous system.

Many authors assert that changes in the development of an idea in creative thought are due to the activity of the unconscious, but they don't actually know if that is true. All that these persons can tell from introspection is what actually occurs in their conscious mind. Such writers are aware of the stage of preparation, in which they have expended much effort working without success, and of illumination, in which the correct idea emerges suddenly with a feeling of elation.

Both of these two stages command attention: preparation because of a sense of perplexity, doubt, and feeling of failure, along with the awareness of prolonged effort and lack of success; illumination because of a sense of relief, of achievement, and of happiness or elation which accompanies it. The stage of incubation, however, is not so obvious, either by a sense of striving and frustration characteristic of the stage of preparation, or by a sense of achievement and elation characteristic of illumination. Often in incubation the subject has temporarily stopped his unsuccessful striving apparent in preparation and has turned to routine activities. Nor is the feeling of achievement and elation present, which is found in illumination, for the idea is not yet modified enough to be the solution of the problem. Hence it is no wonder that these authors are greatly impressed by the stages of preparation and illumination and pass unnoticed over the stage of incubation, in which they are thinking casually about the problem as they engage in other activities. Even the stage of verification attracts more notice than that of incubation, for in this last stage the subject forces himself to pursue a concentrated line of work. It is no wonder then that some of these writers attribute to the working of the unconscious the sudden appearance of the solution in illumination, for they are unaware of the stage of incubation, in which they have casually thought of the idea from time to time as they engage in other matters.

When the poets and artists in Patrick's experiment were questioned about whether or not they incubated the ideas for poems and pictures, they were all aware of it, in the majority of cases. No doubt, if those writers who rely on the subconscious had been so questioned, they would also have been aware of the intermittent recurrence of the idea finally adopted as the solution during incubation. It is only natural, when they are not aware of intervening thoughts and ideas, which connect the stages of preparation and illumination, that the unconscious be invoked as an explanation.

In fact, even if the unconscious were operating, those

persons would not by definition be able to tell that fact from their own introspections.

The exploratory behavior characteristic of the stage of preparation is similar to the exploratory behavior that occurs only in the first trial of trial and error learning *before* the goal is reached. In trial and error learning, on the first trial the blind alleys may be entered more often or less often than the correct alley. Likewise, in creative thought, in preparation and incubation the chief idea which becomes the solution may recur either more often or less often than the rejected ideas. Both for creative thought and for the first trial of trial and error learning the wrong response fails to terminate the need and so permits the appearance of more correct responses, which more adequately terminate the need until the idea of the solution appears.

If a rat were capable of creative thinking and the maze situation in respect to the ability of the rat were difficult enough to induce creative thinking, then the process of creative thought would correspond to *only the first trial* of the learning process. Since the recurrence of the correct idea, as well as of the irrelevant ones, appears in creative thinking *before* the goal or solution is reached, the influence of having reached the goal in stamping in the correct responses on subsequent trials, as in the case of maze learning, does not appear here. In the first trial of typical maze learning *before* the goal is reached, there is a recurrence of both the irrelevant responses and the partially correct response, which is modified to become the correct response when the reward is reached the first time. In creative thinking the correct response shows a tendency to recur before the goal is reached the first time, just as the irrelevant responses do. Creative thinking is reaching a goal or solution for the first time; learning, which involves not only reaching the goal for the first time on the first trial, but also on later trials, is the stamping in of a correct response which has already been achieved. We cannot say that in incubation all of the ideas thought of in preparation have an equal tendency to return, for some ideas are thought of only once in preparation and never recur. Both the correct idea, as well as some irrelevant ones, show a tendency to recur *before* the solution or goal is achieved. Why? Satisfaction or pleasantness from getting the reward does not operate here, for the correct response occurs before the reward is reached. The fact that a solution may be reached before reinforcement can operate has been discussed by Allport. He shows that "insightful solutions must have occurred before they can yield reinforcement or satisfaction."

When a person has an unterminated want as induced by the problem situation a certain unbalanced condition is set up in the nervous system. Some thoughts or neural excitations restore the equilibrium to a greater extent than other thoughts or neural excitations, which have little or no effect on restoring the equilibrium. Since during incubation the given neural excitation (which restores equilibrium to a greater extent than other neural excitations), is not yet modified sufficiently to restore the equilibrium, it passes away temporarily, and when it recurs again this neural excitation has been modified by the fact that it recurs in a different mental set. As it recurs in different mental sets it is further modified until this modified neural excitation restores the equilibrium and the subject experiences the solution characteristic of illumination. The chemical-physical nature of the neural excitation, which is the solution, is of such a nature that it restores the equilibrium in the unbalanced physical-chemical state set up in the nervous system by the unterminated want or need of the problem. This termination of the want or need is correlated on the conscious side with closure and the formation of a new configuration.

The stage of verification consists of many perceptions. The solution obtained in illumination is compared with the standards of art or science, according to the nature of the problem, and if the idea obtained in illumination has been put in definite form, as is typically the case, then perception operates to see if it corresponds to the standards of art or science.

The stage of verification or revision also consists of judgments in addition to perceptions. When the definite form in which the idea or solution has crystallized is compared to the standards of art or science as conceived in the mind of the thinker if the relationship is not immediately obvious, as in perception, then a judgment based on the reasoning process characteristic of simpler situations may be necessary. Thus in trying to decide which of several possible details should be added, the equilibrium in the neural organization of the thinker has been again disturbed. Because of the relative simplicity of the problems found in the stage of verification or revision in deciding about the addition or elimination of details (as compared with the total process of creative thought in which the solution has appeared in the illumination stage after a period of incubation) the equilibrium is more easily restored in each of the minor neural disturbances, which appear during verification.

If the idea which eventually becomes the solution in the stage of illumination has been assembled along with irrelevant material in the stage of preparation, then when the active work on the problem is discontinued during incubation, why does this idea recur from time to time? The mechanism or causes underlying the tendency of the correct idea to recur from time to time during incubation, while the irrelevant ideas may also recur, but are eliminated after obtaining the solution, are similar to those which operate in physical maze learning, in which the partially correct muscular responses leading to the goal, as well as the incorrect ones recur, but the first trial ceases after the reward is reached. Although there are large differences in type of problem and type of response, yet a comparison can be made between the appearance of correct and incorrect responses in maze learning on the first trial and in creative thinking.

Morgan's well-known description of problem solving states that the first requirement is the existence of some motive, need, or urge to activity. In many animal experiments hunger is used as the motive. Second, the animal's motivated behavior is subject to thwarting by some circumstance that prevents the immediate completion of the act. Third, the organism engages in varied responses, or "trial and error," until, fourth, some solution is hit upon which fulfills the original need and completes the sequence of activity. "This analysis—(1) motive (2) thwarting (3) varied responses and (4) solution—applies broadly to the more complicated processes of reasoning, as well as to the simpler explicit forms of problem-solving," according to Shaffer, Gilmer, and Schoen. "A gross analysis of the thinking process has shown that it consists of the suggestion of hypotheses which are criticized and accepted or rejected. In overt problem-solving, as in the solution of a mechanical puzzle, the hypotheses are the 'trials' and are carried out by obvious manual manipulations." In the statement, "In overt problem-solving, as in the solution of a mechanical puzzle, the hypotheses are the 'trials' and are carried out by obvious manual manipulations," the authors do not distinguish between the random trial and error behavior which occurs *before* the solution is reached the first time when the animal in the maze or problem box obtains the food, and the trials which occur *after* the animal has reached the reward and is put in the maze or problem box again. The random behavior which occurs in the "trials" subsequent to reaching the reward the first time is more or less modified by the fact that the reward has actually once been reached. The random behavior which occurs before the goal is reached is not so modified.

When they speak of the analysis: (1) motive (2) thwarting (3) varied responses, and (4) solution applying to the more complicated processes of reasoning, as well as to the simpler explicit forms of problem solving, that is true only in regard to the first trial before the goal is reached. After the reward or solution has once been reached, the comparison between creative thinking and simpler problem solving breaks down. In creative thought after the solution has once been reached, there is no motivation to strive for the same solution again; but in simpler reasoning and overt problem situations the recurrent motivation of physical or social urges prompts the organism to strive for a similar solution when similar problem situations and wants occur. When the animal or subject is placed in a similar situation again, the fact of having once obtained the reward influences the random behavior on the second and subsequent trials in a manner in which it was not influenced on the first trial before the goal had ever been reached. After the reward has been reached the first time (on the first trial) all subsequent trials merely serve to fixate and improve the correct response with practice.

Unfulfilled wants related to physical needs as hunger, thirst, and sex will recur after an interval as strongly as if they hadn't been terminated at all, whereas in the complicated situation of the creative thinker, when once the unterminated want has been fulfilled by the solution to the problem, that particular need will not recur again in the same form. Consequently the animal who has once fulfilled the need for hunger, sex, or thirst can be placed after an interval in the same maze or problem box and have as strong a motivation to solve it as on the first trial, due to the recurrent need of those urges. The record of the animal on succeeding trials in the same maze or problem box can thus be compared, but in the case of the creative thinker, once the unfulfilled want has been ended by the solution to the problem, that particular unterminated want does not recur. When the artist in the stage of illumination conceives the idea for a certain painting or the inventor conceives the idea for a certain machine, the unterminated want for that particular type of art object or machine has been fulfilled and there is no recurrent motivation to induce him to tackle the same problem again, hence no record can be kept of his behavior on subsequent trials, as with the animal in the maze or problem box. Furthermore, the correct response is so forcibly impressed or learned by the thinker in the stage of illumination, that, even if the identical problem occurred again, he would probably make the correct response at once on subsequent occasions. Even animals, who have solved problem boxes by insight, when motivated by recurrent physical needs to solve the same problem again, often display the correct response at once on subsequent trials, showing that the correct response was thoroughly learned on the first trial. Thus many unfulfilled wants, which are induced by physical or social circumstances, may recur repeatedly with the same intensity even after the solution or reward has been obtained on many previous occasions. But in the much more difficult and complicated process of creative thought, the unfulfilled want to create a certain object of art or to obtain a specific scientific discovery or invention does not recur again after that specific solution has been obtained.

In our opinion, the first trial, in both creative thinking and solving maze problems, continues until the reward or solution is reached the first time. This may last a few minutes or hours in the case of the rat, or extend into days and weeks in the case of the thinker. For the rat, until the random movements are followed by reaching the goal the first time, we can't say there was a trial. The unterminated want has not been fulfilled until the reward is reached, hence there has been no trial. Nor can we say that every unsuccessful movement made by a rat on the first trial is in itself a trial, or the first trial would be composed of many unsuccessful trials. If every random movement is to be called a trial, then some word besides "trial" must be used to designate the total activity of reaching the reward and terminating the want. Thus the process of creative thought, with preparation, incubation, and reaching the solution in illumination corresponds to the first trial of learning a maze problem, when the reward or solution is actually reached the first time and the activity is terminated for that trial.

There is knowledge of "purpose," "goal," or "object of desire" if the unfulfilled want is of the nature to be registered in consciousness, as certain physiological processes are not. The awareness of a problem to be solved is the conscious correlate of the disturbance in the equilibrium of the nervous system caused by some stimulus, either internal or external. The idea of "purpose" or "goal to be reached" is merely an inadequate response which only partially fulfills the unterminated want. This inadequate response of purpose or goal is either (a) a specific response or habit learned from solving previous similar problems, or (b) a more generalized response abstracted from many previous responses, as interest or concept, but which is inadequate to complete the unfulfilled want of the present problem. When this insufficient idea first appears in the preparation stage, it initiates various ideas which were previously associated with it. Some of these recur from time to time with modifications as they reappear in different mental sets, as typical of incubation. When the inadequate idea of "purpose" or "goal" has been modified sufficiently to assume a definite form which fulfills the unterminated want and restores the equilibrium in the nervous system, the problem is solved; although new unfulfilled wants immediately arise in the stage of verification, as the solution reached in illumination is compared with the standards of art or science. These minor unfulfilled wants are typically concerned with simpler problems, as the addition or elimination of details, than is true of the want of the main problem just described, which is much more complex.

Rice states, "The purpose is that aspect of the act for the sake of which it is done, that to which satisfaction has attached in the past or to which it attaches by way of anticipation. . . . Our symbol of the purpose intervenes between the stimulus and the overt response. . . . As we are carrying out the successive phases of the act, we keep the symbolized purpose in mind, mull it over, and confirm it repeatedly; unswerving concentration on the purpose, as it begets auxiliary goals, is necessary to keep us going."

According to Rice the symbol of purpose intervenes between the stimulus and the solution response. This occurs because the symbol of purpose is merely an inadequate response which does not fulfill the unterminated want of the problem situation, hence it continues to recur until the solution response restores the equilibrium in the nervous system and the problem is ended. Thus the "symbol of purpose" or "partly adequate response" intervenes between the stimulus and the response, which solves the problem.

As mentioned before, the so-called anticipation of solving a problem is really the satisfaction which accompanied the arousal of an idea of a response which solved a similar problem in the past (although there are some cases when a previous solution is unpleasant). Thus when the subject is first aware of the want or need set up within himself by the problem situation he immediately recalls the solution previously made to a similar problem, with its attendant affective feeling (which is typically pleasant) and he thinks how desirable such a solution would be to solve the present problem. However, this idea of the solution to a problem in the past is inadequate to fulfill the unterminated want of the present problem and the search continues for the specific response which will do so. This anticipation of solving a problem has been referred to as "purpose." As pointed out above, purpose is either a specific response or habit derived from the solution of a number of similar problems in the past, or a more generalized response or interest or concept which has been abstracted from the solutions of many similar problems in the past.

"One useful approach holds that incubation is analogous to a plateau of a learning curve," according to Shaffer, Gilmer, and Schoen. "The facts and observations have all been made during the period of preparation, and have been learned so thoroughly that slight gestures and other imperceptible muscle movements can symbolize them. The thinker need not work systematically during incubation, because he is so thoroughly saturated with his problem that he can reject one hypothesis by a nod of the head and represent another by a shrug of the shoulders. During incubation he is rearranging his ideas by the use of these subtle symbols, just as during a plateau in motor learning a habit is being reorganized on a higher level."

In this analogy it must be remembered that there is a fundamental difference between the plateau in the learning curve and the process of incubation. The learning curve is based on the results of a number of trials as the subject tries to solve the same problem (or very similar problem) again and again. In creative thinking, on the other hand, the problem is only solved once. Incubation thus represents only a part of the first trial, not the results of a number of trials in solving the same problem. As we have shown elsewhere, in incubation the recurrence of the idea which becomes the solution takes place before the solution is reached and the unfulfilled want is terminated, for the first time. The results of the learning curve, however, are derived from the subject reaching the solution and terminating the unfulfilled want of the same problem a number of times. The analogy between incubation and the plateau of the learning curve does not extend very far.

Learning is modification of response by practice and fixation and operates after the goal has been reached the first time and creative thought is over.

In simpler problem situations the unfulfilled want of the problem is terminated the first time the idea of the solution appears. However, in creative thinking, where the difficulty of the problem is much greater in regard to the capacity of the subject, the correct solution may recur from time to time without being accepted, because it has not yet appeared in a form to fulfill the unterminated want of the problem.

It is well known that when an idea has been experienced it has a tendency to recur unless it is inhibited. Both irrelevant and pre-solution ideas show a tendency to recur during preparation and incubation. When an idea recurs it must necessarily be in a different mental set for consciousness is a process and no two configurations are ever exactly the same. Both irrelevant and pre-solution ideas are modified by the different configurations in which they occur. As the pre-solution idea recurs in different mental sets with modifications it is still inadequate to terminate the unfulfilled want of the problem. Finally it appears in the form in which the unterminated want of the problem situation is fulfilled, the equilibrium in the nervous system is restored, and the solution is reached.

When writing a poem, why do only the experiences connected with such literary activity come into play instead of past experiences in regard to arithmetic and breakfast food, for instance? Since the unfulfilled want of any problem situation is similar to other wants which the thinker has experienced, habits which have previously been built up as solutions to similar wants are called into play. Entirely unrelated responses do not usually occur. These habitual solutions to similar previous wants do not terminate the unfulfilled want of the present problem situation and additional perceptions and ideas obtained from the environment are merged into the background of these habitual responses in imaginative activity. Extraneous ideas entirely unrelated to the previous solutions of similar wants are not usually evoked.

All responses, both incorrect, which are later discarded, and partially correct, which later become the solution after modification, are supplanted by other responses as long as the unterminated want of the problem situation remains. As long as a person is alive, his ideas and mental processes are constantly changing, and as long as the unterminated want of the problem situation persists, various responses related to that want, as determined by the person's past experiences, will continue to recur.

When the thinker lays the problem aside and turns his attention to other matters temporarily, the partially correct idea, which eventually becomes the solution, recurs from time to time with modifications as it appears in different mental sets. But it must also be remembered that ideas which fail to become the solution also reappear from time to time with modifications in different mental sets. In other words the inadequate responses (both the one which eventually becomes the correct response and the ones that do not) are modified by the perceptions, interests, attitudes, and mental sets associated with the different activities, which the thinker assumes when he ceases work on the problem. Thus, even though the thinker lays the problem aside and ceases to think about it, as he did in the preparation stage when he was working on it with deliberate, voluntary effort, yet the fact that he reconsiders it from time to time while he is doing other things shows that the unterminated want reappears at intervals while he is engaged in other activities. As long as the unfulfilled want of the problem situation persists, it will recur from time to time, even though it is inhibited from appearing continuously by the other wants of daily living.

The unfulfilled want or need is represented in consciousness by an unpleasant affective state as long as it is not terminated during preparation and incubation. In illumination, when the solution appears, a feeling of satisfaction and elation is evident. The pleasant affective state characteristic of illumination is often in turn superseded by an affective state in the verification stage, which is less pleasant and involves doubt and criticism, as new unsatisfied wants arise when the subject compares his idea of a solution with the standards of art or science as he conceives them. These minor disturbances in the equilibrium of the nervous system are in turn usually satisfied by simpler reasoning responses and judgments.

The protocols obtained by Patrick, Duncker, Christof

and Claparede in separate experiments, show the recurrence of the idea which becomes the solution, as well as the reappearance of those which are discarded.

Summary

The explanation of incubation in terms of the subconscious mind is discussed. Other interpretations in terms of rest and different mental sets are presented. The Gestalt description of thinking is given. A problem situation induces an unfulfilled want in the organism which is accompanied by a disturbance of equilibrium in the nervous system and which is registered in consciousness by the awareness of the problem. The solution is the response with its accompanying neural correlate which terminates the want and restores the equilibrium in the nervous system. It is registered in consciousness by the awareness that the problem has been solved. Creative thought corresponds to the first trial of the learning process. Reaching the solution in illumination corresponds to reaching the reward or goal for the first time (on the first trial of the learning process). Factors involved in the reappearance of the chief idea in incubation are: 1. In the stage of preparation ideas determined by past experience are aroused which are related to the fulfillment of the unterminated want of the problem situation. Entirely unrelated ideas do not usually appear. 2. If an idea has occurred once, it has a tendency to recur. 3. The ideas aroused in preparation have a tendency to recur, the irrelevant ideas as well as the partially correct ones, but none of them adequately fulfills the unterminated want. 4. The correct idea (which eventually becomes the solution) in its original form may fail to adequately fulfill the unterminated want, and is superseded by irrelevant ideas. 5. As the pre-solution idea recurs in different mental sets it is modified, even as the incorrect ideas are modified as they recur. 6. When the correct idea finally recurs in the form to terminate the unfulfilled want, illumination occurs and the solution is reached. 7. The stage of verification follows in which the solution is compared to the standards of art or science. New problems involving untermi- nated wants appear, but they involve simpler processes of perception and judgment than the more difficult problem of creative thought. The idea of "purpose," "goal" or "object of desire" is a response which has been made to a similar problem or problems in the past, but which is inadequate to restore the equilibrium in the nervous system induced by the present problem situation. It recurs from time to time with modifications until the solution is reached.

6

EMOTION IN CREATIVE THOUGHT

EMOTION or feeling, of greater or less intensity, often accompanies creative thinking. The type and extent of the affective reaction varies in the different stages.

Capacity for Emotion or Affective Tendency

Various investigators have noted the importance of the affective reaction in the thinking process. Spearman emphasized this by saying, "Even now we have not yet got back to what, in a way, is the most indispensable preliminary of all. This is not a cognitive process of any order, first, second, or third. It is the capacity for and experience of emotion." Similarly, Rignano mentions the great importance of capacity for duration and resistance of the affective tendency if coherence is to be kept during the long process of reasoning. If primary affectivity is necessary for abundance of imagined combinations, secondary affectivity for its part is no less necessary in order to keep the whole reasoning process in continuous and actual correspondence with the real, and thus to guarantee its logicality. The affective activity is the "sole architect which creates every edifice of reasoning."

Among those who stress the importance of emotion in creative thought is Ribot, who states that emotion "is the ferment without which no creation is possible!" Morris asserts that aesthetic purpose is "simply determinate feeling."

"Many great creative artists have testified to the sovereign importance of this element of feeling," according to Rees, who presents a quotation from Rodin: " 'If I have expressed certain feelings in my works, it is utterly useless for me to try to put them into words, for I am not a poet, but a sculptor, and they ought to be easily read in my statues; if not, I might as well not have experienced the feelings.' " Rees concludes, "The artist's emotion is objectified in the final product; a picture, a statue, a musical composition, a poem, or a dance expresses not merely an idea, but the artist's feeling about that idea. If that element is lost, there is not creative artistic expression. . . . Productivity without the artist's emotional reaction is no longer art; emotion links the self of the creator with experience through the senses."

Harding emphasizes the emotional factor by asserting, "Although inspiration can occur to anyone, it will only be manifested in its highest degree in those persons who are capable of this emotional tension." The personal experience of Tschaikowsky[1] is recorded as follows: "It would be in vain for me to endeavor to express in words that immeasurable sense of happiness which comes over me when a new thought appears and begins to grow into definite forms. I then forget everything, and behave as if I were mad; all in me pulsates and vibrates; scarcely have I begun the sketches when thousands of details are chasing each other through my brain."

"Unquestionably in all creative effort there is a decided emotional tone," Rossman writes. "The arousal of insight and its consummation in a practical solution are favored by emotional, temperamental, and mental factors—those which in effect constitute the total personality," according to Alpert.

Different degrees of affectivity may accompany creative thought as Langfeld emphasizes, "While the inspiration to creative effort is an emotional experience, and while this emotional state may recur at intervals during the period of

[1] See Rees (155)

production, for the most part the creative work is carried on with great favor, and in a calm, controlled, and relatively unemotional state of mind. In short, an emotional reaction seems a necessary characteristic, but not a constantly present factor of artistic production." Likewise, Kris points out that the "individual may be elated or depressed, extremely vital or ill." Patrick found from her study of poets and artists that while a majority of both groups speak of being more or less emotionally disturbed while composing, a fifth assert that they usually compose in a detached objective manner.

The influence of personal emotional experiences on artistic production is indicated by Portnoy. "Art creation is the conversion of human emotions which, fed by anxiety, apprehension, longing and anticipation seek and find release in expression. . . . Art is rooted in experience and human emotion." "Early experiences, emotionally colored, are sources of later poetical moments, repeating the emotion; and 'feeling' comes in aid of feeling," according to Prescott. "Thus the great poet must be one who has had a full and fortunate life—and particularly a rich and favorable emotional development in childhood and youth." Likewise Finck[1] mentions, "The living quality of art springs from the emotional reaction of the artist to life."

A study to show "the influence of the affective processes of the personality on the reasoning processes," was made by Lefford. The method consisted of presenting a test of syllogistic problems which were judged for validity and truth. The syllogisms were of two kinds, equated as to structure and length, but differing in the nature of the subject matter: half were concerned with controversial matters likely to arouse some affective response, and half of a neutral nature. "The results confirm what observation of everyday behavior and other studies indicate. It was found that most subjects solve neutrally toned syllogisms more correctly than emotionally toned syllogisms, and that there was little relation-

[1] Rees (155)

ship between the ability to reason accurately in non-emotional and emotional situations."

On the other hand, Wertheimer asserts, "The role of the merely subjective interests of the self is, I think, much overestimated in human actions. Real thinkers forget about themselves in thinking. The main vectors in genuine thought often do not refer to the I with its personal interests; rather, they represent the structural requirements of the given situation. Or when such vectors do refer to an I, this is not just the I as center of subjective striving." "In human terms there is at bottom the desire, the craving to face the true issue, the structural core, the radix of the situation; to go on from an unclear, inadequate relation to a clear, transparent, direct confrontation—straight from the heart of the thinker to the heart of his object, of his problem. All the items hold also for real attitudes and for action, just as they do for thinking processes. And thinking processes of this type themselves involve real attitudes."

A stifling of creative thinking may have an adverse effect on the personality, according to Hutchinson. When the creative desire is stifled "the hidden enterprise bobs up in hydra-headed forms producing sometimes melancholy, anxiety, fatigue, inflation of ego, sometimes over-idealization of purpose. . . . There seems to be little question that prolonged, enforced repression of the creative desire may lead to actual breakdown of the personality. . . . The stifling of creative interests is no incidental matter; it cuts at the very roots of satisfaction in living." "When the creative desire is active, intense, aroused, but for the time restricted in expression, the chief psychological symptom is tension."

Preparation

Hutchinson says that the period of preparation is characterized by random effort and real, vivid and undermining frustration. The initial phase may be quiet or frenzied, according to Portnoy. Christof has shown that thinking begins in bafflement and search for the correct idea.

The stage of preparation is characterized by perplexity and doubt. The subject feels the urge to obtain a solution to a perplexing problem but is unable to do so. Various ideas occur to mind which are untenable and the subject discards them while looking for others. Thus an inventor may want to create a machine to accomplish a certain purpose. He may work for weeks or months gathering information about different kinds of apparatus. Uncertainty, doubt and a rising sense of failure add to the emotional tension.

This stage is frequently unpleasant because of the hard and difficult labor involved. Weeks, months, or even years of painstaking, accurate work may be necessary, as when a scientist is trying to solve a difficult problem. He may spend day after day reading technical journals in order to amass as much information as possible. Hour after hour may be consumed in long, detailed surveys. The lack of apparent progress and the prolonged detailed work may make the stage of preparation a monotonous one. As the thinker labors day after day without apparent progress, he may become greatly discouraged.

Intense and keen frustration may characterize this first period. For instance, an artist may have an idea which he wishes to express. He thinks of various types and groups of figures which would possibly portray his idea. He may seek help by studying the work of other artists as portrayed in books or museums. His feeling of frustration may increase as day after day he fails to find the means of expressing his idea.

Thus the stage of preparation is frequently unpleasant for the thinker. The hard work, which appears to produce no result, is often discouraging. In fact, many times this work is so unpleasant that he abandons the whole problem. Most of the great discoveries in science have previously been attempted by others, who grew so discouraged in the unpleasant first stage that they abandoned the problem without making any further attempts. Many questions, which have led to great discoveries, have frequently been asked by different people, but the unpleasant difficult work of the preparation stage prevented them from reaching a solution.

Incubation

The stage of incubation appears as restless and poorly coördinated activity accompanied by a feeling of unease sometimes approaching misery, according to Shaffer, Gilmer and Schoen. A writer may pace the floor, scribble a few lines and throw them away, become irritable with his family, smoke too many cigarettes, and succumb too readily to passing distractions. His feeling tone is depressed and he is wrought up emotionally. Such a period of incubation often ends in an inspiration or sudden solution of the difficulty.

Hutchinson says that during this second period of "renunciation or recession" the problem is given up in sheer defense of emotional balance and other activities are interpolated. There is a rising emotional tone, restlessness, feeling of inferiority, and a temporary cessation of effort. In this period, if the problem is not settled, strain is evident. "Mild psychoneurotic symptoms appear." The intuitive thinker has a problem-generated neurosis or tension, owing to the practical block to his creative desire. It "involves the tendencies toward repression of the creative problem and dissociation of it from normal consciousness; regression; compensatory reactions; emotional excess." These symptoms relieve tension and reduce the intensity of the creative drive, "forcing it to a temporary state of impotence. The productive process is thrown back on the natural capacity of integration operating in periods of relaxation." There "can be a deliberate attempt to systematize the creative process by setting aside the problem for a planned interval, with the intention of consciously resuming it at a later date." It does not matter if it keeps recurring to consciousness. In the ablest minds the tensions are managed by resigning from the problem for a while.

Although the incubation stage is not characterized by the prolonged effort and strenuous labor of preparation, yet it also is usually accompanied by an unpleasant affective state. It is not so obvious as preparation because the thinker has put aside the problem for a while.

During incubation the thinker may feel uneasy and under a strain. He may exhibit restless behavior and pace the floor, or engage in other uncorrelated acts. He experiences a feeling of tension. This may take expression in unusual irritability toward persons with whom he is associated. He may be surprised at finding himself annoyed at things which don't usually distract him.

Even though he has temporarily quit working on the problem for a while, yet is he still bothered by it. He still keeps thinking about it from time to time in spite of himself. He may engage in some compensatory activity or physical exercise, as a rapid walk, to escape from his thoughts for a while. He may work hard at some manual labor, attempt a different type of mental work, or participate in some form of recreation in order to attain mental relief.

A feeling of fatigue may be evident. The thinker may be both mentally and physically tired to a greater extent than usual. Although he is not engaged in the active labor of the preparation stage, yet he finds that he feels generally tired. The recreational activities in which he participates while he is not working on the problem, do not give him the customary relaxation.

A sense of anxiety frequently pervades this period of creative thought. Although the thinker makes a deliberate effort to put the problem aside, he is worried about his inability to solve it. Even when he is not working on the problem, this feeling of anxiety continues to persist.

While the incubation stage is typically unpleasant, yet, on the other hand, the thinker may notice some improvement as the ideas recur to him from time to time. He may thus be encouraged to some extent.

Illumination

The incubation stage, however, is not characterized by the feeling of pleasure and joy so often found in illumination. Portnoy describes how this stage "finds the artist in his glory." He reaches this period full of emotion, ecstatic and rich in creative ideas. The symptoms vary only in degree with a true artistic personality. Tschaikowsky,[1] speaking of his own experience, says, "If the soil is ready—that is to say if the disposition for the work is there—it takes root with extraordinary force . . . that immeasurable sense of bliss that comes over me directly a new idea awakens in me and begins to assume a definite form." The feeling of elation is emphasized by Snyder, who states that this phase is accompanied "by intense emotional susceptibility common in ecstatic trance" and by "a heightening of the poetic faculty at least proportional to the completeness with which it is focused on one topic."

"When the artist grasps a new vision, he feels like the pioneer and the discoverer which he unquestionably is," writes Feibleman. "He has had a new revelation and his state for the moment is one of unspeakable joy. It is something like that divine madness of which the ancients spoke, a period of quick insight, galvanic action and high excitement for the artist. . . . The witness of artists concerning this stage in the artistic process is not far to seek. We have abundant evidence at hand of what it feels like to be inspired in this particular fashion. Perhaps the most graphic descriptions come from two composers, Mozart and Beethoven. Mozart, for instance, declared that he did not hear the separate parts of a musical composition (which after all take some time in order to be played) one at a time and successively but rather all together ('gleich alles zusammen'), and Beethoven

1 Rees (155)

confirmed this by declaring that the artist sees his whole composition in a single projection ('in einem Gusse').''

Delacroix points out that inspiration is a shock, as an emotion, as the attention suddenly becomes fascinated; it is a flowering. The composer often works in such a feverish state that the hand cannot keep up with the thought, according to Galli.

Some sudden stimulus, coming into a period of slight mental preoccupation after a period of rest, ends the psychic tension during the stage of incubation and precipitates the period of insight, according to Hutchinson. There is a reorganization of the perceptual field, a new alignment of possible hypotheses. There is an "almost hallucinatory vividness of the ideas appearing in connection with any sense department," emotional release, feeling of exultation, adequacy, finality. The individual steps up to a new level of activity and new possibility of reaction. "Exhilaration marks such moments of insight." There is sensory, motor, and emotional experience. The thinker sees a sketch or picture; he moves or shouts; the emotions are quickened. "Artists literally fall in love with their works, thinking they have created a masterpiece." Persons in a laboratory solving a puzzle also laugh and act in triumph. "If one had the least vestige of superstition, it is easy to see how he might suppose himself to be merely the incarnation, merely the mouthpiece, merely the medium of higher forces. It is the impersonality and automatic production of such moments of inspiration that has led to endless theories of extra-personal revelation."

"Familiar objects in a new organization become new things. This is a jolt and gives us the experience we call insight," Maier asserts. "Because new combinations of past experience change the meaning of all parts, we can account for the surprise and thrill which accompanies the solution. . . . It is rather characteristic of great discoveries to appear when they are not being sought." Likewise, Durkin noted excitement, elation, and sometimes relief in her description of sudden reorganization. Henry observed "a feeling of surety and confidence" in insight. In his experiment the subject showed some elation at the discovery of a possibility of solution. The "process of analysis, of 'seeing through a thing' is a very distinct experience," as Ruger points out. In many cases it was a sudden transformation, a "flash" experience. Ogden notes, "It is not the feeling itself that makes insight, but the feeling that this concrete thing belongs to that concrete thing in the process of behavior."

Illumination is especially distinguished by the elation or joy which frequently accompanies it. This feeling of happiness is usually so marked that it attracts the attention of the thinker. When persons are asked to describe their experience as to how they reached a conclusion or produced a work of art, they speak chiefly of this stage and overlook the others to a large extent. In fact, those instances where a person experiences a sudden "vision," or "supernatural" revelation, are due to the fact that the thinker is so impressed with the elation which he feels in this stage that he remembers it and forgets about the unpleasant stages of preparation and incubation which preceded it, and the revision or verification which followed it. It is only natural to remember the experiences which bring us joy and forget those which don't, so the "vision" or "inspiration" which brought us happiness is remembered as an isolated experience, which appeared without previous cause, from some "power" outside of us.

A feeling of relief is evident in this stage. We are all familiar with the classical example of Archimedes, who shouted "Eureka!" as he suddenly thought of the principle of the lever while taking his bath. When a person has worked long and hard during the stage of preparation, and been under a tension during the period of incubation, the "hunch" for a solution or a work of art is accompanied by a great feeling of relief.

Many have observed that the ideas which appear in illumination, are unusually clear and vivid. The idea for a solution or the outline or main structure for a work of art appears sharp and distinct to the thinker, even though many details may be lacking. Sometimes even details are evident and may appear with hallucinatory vividness, as in those instances where the thinker has a "vision." Many have testified as to the clarity of the ideas which have appeared during illumination or "inspiration" as they term it.

The idea which appears in illumination is typically accompanied by a feeling of confidence that it is the right one. The thinker feels sure that it is correct, and that he has hit upon the solution at last. A sense of adequacy and finality is apparent. The thinker is certain that at last he has found the solution to his difficult problem. This feeling of confidence may disappear to some extent during the following stage of verification or revision, but it is very marked during illumination.

The emotional reaction evident in illumination may vary all the way from intense emotional excitement to a mild, pleasant feeling, or indifference. As a rule there is a certain amount of affectivity to a greater or less degree, according to the type and difficulty of the problem, and the personality of the thinker. There are some poets, artists, and composers who assert that they are quite calm and undisturbed during this period. Many, however, speak of an emotional reaction and some to an extreme degree. Not only the artist, but also the scientist, may experience an affective reaction during illumination.

The idea for the solution or work of art, which is evident in this stage, often appears to be unfamiliar to the thinker, as though he had never thought of such a thing before. It has a sense of novelty about it, as something which he had not experienced in other situations. The idea stands out as something new.

Many persons have testified that the ideas, which they receive in illumination, seem to come from some supernatural power. The novelty and unfamiliarity of the idea makes the thinker believe that it could not have originated in his own mental processes. Therefore he may believe that it comes from some power outside of himself. He may attribute it to a spirit of one sort or another, depending on his cultural background. Or he may resort to some form of clairvoyance or thought transference as the explanation. A mystical interpretation in terms of outside influence is often emphasized by artists, writers, musicians and others, because it increases their sense of importance. If they have a mystical "inspiration," which the average person lacks, it increases their prestige in the social group in which they live. As a result they are permitted certain privileges and exemptions from customary rules of conduct on account of their poetic, artistic, or musical "temperament." The average person is willing to accept the description of mystical inspirations of famous persons, since their work is superior to his own. He does not realize that his own creative thinking shows the same essential stages of that of the great man of letters, although the results of his thinking have much less social value.

Revision or Verification

The final stage of revision or verification is typically unpleasant and involves prolonged, hard work. Shaffer, Gilmer and Schoen emphasize this when they write, "In the final period of verification, the creative process again settles down to hard labor. The scientist who has conceived a brilliant hypothesis must test it by further experiments, comparisons, or calculations. . . . The labor of verification is present in the fine arts as well as in the sciences. The painter must transfer his inspiration to the canvas, and the musician work out his broad conception in terms of melodies and harmonies. In literature there is ample evidence of deliberate revision and elaboration before a poem or an essay is finally acceptable to its writer. Manuscripts of great authors show much crossing out and interpolation. The final stage of writing is not an easy task, even for those who are most able."

Similarly Hartmann emphasizes the work involved. In art the final stage "corresponds to the polishing stage—the initial rough design is smoothed and refined into the best possible form. In science and conduct of a 'practical' sort, the illumination is not a final guide to action until objective tests and checks in the laboratory or in the field have confirmed its correctness." "Nearly everyone has seen some artist at work, writing down words or notes, carving in stone, or painting on canvas," according to Feibleman.

The emotional difference between the third and fourth stages is emphasized by Hutchinson. "Insight releases new energies, verification consumes that energy."

After the happiness and elation evident in illumination, the last stage of verification or revision stands in contrast, because it is so often very unpleasant. Prolonged hard work is the outstanding characteristic of this period. The thinker may work days, months, or even years to revise or verify his production. Prolonged attention to minute details, which is necessary for elaboration, adds to the unhappiness of the thinker. In order to revise and verify his work he may have to read extensively or conduct extensive tests to check or re-check his results. He may spend many tedious hours acquiring more information about the standards of his branch of art or science, so that he can modify his own product to conform to those standards. The extensive detailed labor required to carry out the implications of the solution or to complete the outline for a work of art is often very unpleasant. The thinker's unhappiness may last many times longer than the elation of the brief illumination stage. This unpleasantness may range from a small degree of affectivity to great depression.

The thinker feels that his work does not measure up to his expectations. The idea which appeared so worthwhile in illumination now seems to be full of defects. As the thinker works, he observes more imperfections of which he was not aware at first. The artist realizes that his picture, statue, poem or composition does not produce the effect which he had intended. Often he is at a loss to determine why, and his dissatisfaction remains, without being able to remedy the situation. Frequently much work is necessary to enable the artist to ascertain why his product lacks merit. The same is true in scientific work. Dissatisfaction often accompanies the unpleasantness engendered by the tedious labor of revision and verification.

The feeling of confidence engendered in illumination may disappear. As the thinker becomes engrossed in revision and verification, he grows much less certain of his success. During most of this period he lacks the self-assurance which he had in the preceding stage, as he becomes more aware of the defects and imperfections in his work. However, near the end of the period of verification or revision the thinker's self-confidence returns, as he completes his work and views it in final form.

Much great work has never been completed because of the discouragement inherent in this fourth stage. Many excellent ideas have fallen by the wayside because the thinker never carried out the hard extensive work necessary to complete them. Many of the principles underlying famous inventions or discoveries in science have been conceived at various times in the past, but the thinker lacked the perseverance to carry them out to final form, and so they were overlooked or forgotten. No matter how brilliant a "hunch" a person might happen to have, it loses much of its effectiveness if adequate revision and verification are lacking. Many persons become so discouraged in this final stage that they either abandon the whole project or else produce a second rate product.

Creative Thinking of the Psychopath

As many investigators have noted, the illumination stage is usually accompanied by a distinct sense of pleasure, of greater or less intensity. Frequently elation and joy are evident. After a person has struggled and worried trying to solve a difficult problem for a long time, he experiences great happiness when he hits upon an answer in the stage of illumination. It gives him great relief to find an answer at last. The hunch comes as an abrupt, joyful termination to his previous worry and distress.

The psychopathic individual is one who has experienced severe conflict. He has been faced with a difficult problem in life, which he has been unable to solve. Much worry and strenuous effort have accompanied his efforts to find a solution to the complicated situation, which has confronted him. He has been distressed and unhappy for a long time trying to find a means of escape from the complicated circumstances in which he has been placed. Hence, when the tension and unhappiness of the stages of preparation and incubation are suddenly terminated in the idea for a solution in the period of illumination, the thinker is elated. He experiences joy and profound relief that at last he has obtained an answer to his problem.

The psychotic individual has a strong feeling of confidence in this solution, which he has suddenly found to end all his troubles. He is sure it is the correct one. The feeling of certainty in regard to the solution is very marked. He unquestionably accepts it and dwells upon it with great pleasure. He thinks about it often and he likes to dream about the way he has found an answer to his problem. His elation and confidence in that solution, which he has finally reached in the problem which caused him so much misery, prompts him to meditate and dream about it, often for hours at a time.

This "wonderful" idea gives him so much pleasure after his severe unhappiness that the psychopathic individual clings to it and is loath to undergo the discouragement inherent in the final stage of revision or verification. He shrinks away from testing his solution in accordance with the facts of reality. He cannot bring himself to face the fact that his solution is actually inadequate. Consequently he clings to the erroneous idea and spends many hours elaborating it instead of revising and verifying it according to the facts of reality. He works out elaborate and detailed plans, all of which are based on the erroneous solution which he has failed to verify. Psychopathic delusions are highly complex systems of thought which are based on wrong ideas which do not accord with reality. The delusions may be logical developments, but since they are based on the wrong solutions or premises, they do not correspond with actual conditions.

The lack of verification or revision, then, is the chief difference between psychotic imaginative thinking and the creative thought of the average person. This fourth stage is the chief factor which distinguishes both psychopathic daydreaming and ordinary reverie from productive creative thought. It is this final stage that links the creative thought of the individual with the facts of reality and the cultural environment in which he lives. When it is lacking we find the eccentricities and absurdities characteristic of both psychopathic thinking and ordinary reverie. When the productive creative thinker, on the other hand, tests his solution in the fourth stage he becomes aware of its accuracy and validity. If he finds it is defective and out of touch with reality he discards the whole concept, and either abandons the problem completely or begins a new process of creative thought.

Even psychopathic thinking of the depressed type may also be derived from an idea which originally brought pleasure to the patient. As he elaborates and meditates on the consequences of what was originally a pleasant idea, he may become very depressed. If the original idea, which brought pleasure, had been checked with reality in the fourth stage of revision or verification, the patient would not be so depressed out of all proportion to his environment. The reason the patient's depression is so exaggerated in accordance with reality is that his thinking is out of touch with his environment. Although at first the erroneous idea or premise may have been a welcome relief which brought pleasure to the patient after his conflict, yet the detailed elaboration of it may later bring depression.

Summary

The stage of preparation is typically accompanied by an unpleasant affective state of doubt and uncertainty, which may also involve a sense of failure. Prolonged, difficult or detailed work to obtain information about the problem often adds to the unpleasantness of this period. There is a definite sense of frustration. As the preparation stage is prolonged the thinker may become discouraged and sometimes abandons the problem entirely.

The period of incubation may likewise be unpleasant, even though the thinker has ceased the active, strenuous effort evident in preparation. A feeling of tension and excessive irritability may be present. Unusual fatigue and a sense of anxiety may add to the unpleasantness of this stage. The thinker may engage in various activities, as physical exercise, recreation, or other types of work.

The stage of illumination is distinguished from the two preceding periods by the pleasure or elation which frequently accompanies it. A sense of relief and a feeling of confidence are characteristic. The ideas during illumination or "inspiration" are unusually clear and vivid. The novelty and unfamiliarity of the ideas may cause the thinker to believe they came from some power outside himself. The assumption that the great creative thinker has mystical inspiration, which the average person lacks, increases the prestige of the former in the social group.

The final stage of verification or revision is typically unpleasant, often to a marked degree, because of the long, hard, or detailed labor involved. Dissatisfaction and a lack of confidence are often evident as the thinker becomes more aware of the defects and imperfections in his work. The thinker may become so discouraged in his efforts that he either abandons the whole project or else produces a second rate result.

However, the dissatisfaction and lack of confidence evident in the early part of this stage may disappear entirely as the thinker brings his work to successful completion.

The psychotic individual is one who has been very distressed and unhappy trying to solve a difficult problem with which he has been confronted. Hence, when the tension of the stages of preparation and incubation is suddenly terminated in illumination, he experiences joy and profound relief that at last he has obtained an answer to his problem. He clings to his solution and is loath to undergo the discouragement inherent in the final stage of revision and verification. Instead of testing his solution in accordance with the facts of reality he clings to the erroneous solution and spends many hours elaborating it. The lack of verification or revision is the chief factor which differentiates both psychopathic daydreaming and ordinary reverie from productive creative thought.

7

IMAGINATION AND CREATIVE THOUGHT

Fusion of Images Or Elements of Past Experience

THE importance of imagination in productive thought
has been emphasized by a number of writers. It has been
variously described as the fusion of images or elements of
past experience into new combinations.

Binet long ago wrote, "Three images which succeed each
other, the first evoking the second by resemblance, and the
second suggesting the third by contiguity—that is reasoning."

Hobbes, Locke, Hume, Mill, and Spencer expounded
Associationism. Watt and Ach of the Wurzburg group re-
tained association as the basic mechanism of thought, but it
was supplemented by "aufgabe" or determining tendency.
"The classical association theory claims that if two experiences occur together, and one of them later recurs, the
other is reinstated. Watt and Ach claim that out of many
candidates for reinstatement the relevant one is selected by
means of some extra-associational factor," according to
Humphrey. "Associational psychology derived both energy
and relevance from the single principle of association, or in
the later terminology, from the reproductive tendencies,"
and "explained their relevance by the Aufgabe and determining tendencies."

Thinking and reasoning "show the action of the simple
general laws of connecting in cases where the connections

are with elements of the situation rather than with gross totals, and where the connections compete and coöperate in subtle and complicated organizations," according to Thorndike. "A quantitative difference in associative learning is by this theory the producer of the qualitative differences which we call powers of ideation, analysis, abstract and general notions, inference, and reasoning."

"A perception arouses a thought, this thought excites another thought, this in turn a third and so on. A long series of thoughts may arise in quick succession. Such a train of thoughts is called thinking," write Warren and Carmichael. "The succession of mental images and thoughts is commonly called association of ideas." Likewise Pyle asserts, "Reasoning is the flow of ideas evoked by a new situation or partially new."

The fruitfulness of reasoning depends on imagination being not only reproductive but productive—recombining old elements, as Rignano suggests. The fusion of images or elements of past experience into new combinations has been indicated by Pillsbury, when he says that inference or deriving a conclusion always depends on the laws of association. Miller states that thinking is a stream of images organized in such a way as to perform the function of consciously adjusting means to ends, through the activity of the imagination.

The function of thought is "a subjective reproduction of objective experiences, in which orientation in the past is co-existent with and guided by a large amount of orientation in the present," according to Rosett. Hargreaves has analyzed imagination into fluency and originality. Fluency was reduced to speed or quickness, memory, and an unknown factor; originality was reduced to memory, an element common to fluency, and an unknown factor described as a cognitive-conative process.

Prescott describes imagination by saying, "The ingredient images are not merely juxtaposed or even combined; they rather coalesce, one image, or features from it, running into another, and all growing together, by an organic action of the mind." They thus form a composite unity, related to its many constituent elements, but essentially a new creation. "Poetic or mystic visions, daydreams, hypnagogic visions, dreams, illusions and hallucinations, whether normal or abnormal—are in character alike. In all the essence is in the visionary action of the mind. One therefore may explain another; and all may help to explain the working of the poetic imagination." "The pictures presented by the poetic imagination in its sudden vision must often be worked over and connected by ordinary thought to take their place in the poem."

Ribot points out, "In order that a creative act occur, there is required, first, a need; then, that it arouse a combination of images; and lastly, that it objectify and realize itself in an appropriate form. . . . The non-imaginative person is such from lack of materials or through the absence of resourcefulness." "One of the best conditions for inventing is an abundance of material, accumulated experience. . . . The combining imagination joined to the inductive spirit constitutes 'the talent for invention strictly so-called' in industry, science, artist, and poet." "The so-called creative imagination surely proceeds in very different ways, according to temperament, aptitudes, and in some individuals, following the mental disposition, the milieu." Man creates because of needs and desires, and because of "spontaneous revival of images grouped in new combinations." The creative imagination is the property of images to gather in new combinations.

"The imagination . . . the true inward creatrix, instantly out of the chaos of elements or shattered fragments of memory, puts together some form to fit it," in the opinion of Lowes. "For that aimless flow of associations from 'the twilight realms of consciousness' is, when uncurbed, the bane of all those who, like Coleridge himself, are what he called 'reverie-ish and streamy.' Yet it is also that very flux of interweaving phantasms of association which, when the creative energy imposes its will upon it, becomes the plastic stuff both of life and of art." "Conceptions of the nature of imagination vary from definition as the simple reproduction and reconstruction of sense material by the use of imagery" through other definitions and descriptions to views of creativity as an instinct, according to Markey.

Redintegration, Constellation, and Complex

Hollingworth has shown that the world of reverie is complex and involves many associations. He notes how cues redintegrate old patterns or predispose towards one rather than another new pattern. In random thinking, only one cue is required at a time, but in reflective thought at least two cues are required. The one is the present detail that functions in redintegrating a consequent event or in mere associative reproduction. The other cue is the second detail that determines the course of redintegration.

In [1]Muller's theory of constellation, if some associative traces are connected to the problem situation (S) and others to the response (P), the one connected to both S and P appears and others are lost. Selz asserts that the selective process is not exploration of the constellation of ideas or trial and error elimination. On the contrary it is immediate and direct and has many aspects of possible reflex action. Associationism is not conducive because it fails to redintegrate the elements to give unity. Selz differs from association theories in that the solution is not based on isolated parts and their isolated associated traces, but is at once anticipatorily related by certain general relations to the whole complex. He advocates the complex theory. Schema has been used by Selz, Betz and Flach to indicate the character of a blank form or scheme to be filled out.

Eduction of a Correlate

"Both artistic and scientific thinking attain their supreme degree of creativity by virtue of the process which has

[1] Duncker (37)

been called the educing of a 'correlate,' " suggests Spearman.
"The final act in creativity must be assigned to the third
neogenetic process; that of displacing a relation from the
ideas which were its original fundaments to another idea,
and thereby generating the further idea which is correlative
to the last named, and which may be entirely novel."

Differences between the Gestalt group and the Spearman
group have been discussed by Woodworth. "While the two
have not come to grips on precisely this question, it is certain
that Spearman speaks of the seeing, or 'eduction' of relations and correlates as the essence of intellectual activity,
whereas the Gestalt group emphasizes organized wholes, total patterns. A pattern includes relations as 'dependent
parts,' but is not composed of relations, being psychologically
prior to relations, in the Gestalt view." Underwood states
that creative thinking requires "the recognition or learning
of relationships among relationships."

Gestalt or Configuration

Wheeler writes from the Gestalt point of view when he
notes that associationism does "not explain what makes a
train of thought go on and what finally terminates it." According to the configurationists, "a given thought process is
an organized response from its beginning to its end. . . .
The perception of a problem is a directional activity proceeding by virtue of its own organization, toward a goal, and
the thought process is not complete until the goal is reached."
He believes there is no conflict between the facts of thinking
as described by association and configuration. The conflict
is only in the theory. "The two accounts are supplementary
when the data of the introspectionist are treated in the light
of configurational principles."

The Gestalt viewpoint is also indicated by Maier. "The
concept of equivalent stimuli has added much to our understanding of the way in which past experience influences subsequent behavior. When old experiences influence the be-

havior in novel situations, it is because the new situation contains (for the individual in question) an element or relationship to which the person has previously learned to react. . . . In order to understand the process of productive thinking, it is first necessary to distinguish between situations in which subjective identity in past learning and the demands of the problem are present at the outset, and situations in which the identity must be achieved by alterations in past experience. This distinction is implied when one uses the term reproductive thinking to designate problems solved by the process of equivalent stimuli and the term productive thinking to designate problems solved by processes which involve changes or a restructuring in past experience. . . . Once we recognize that the mechanism of equivalent stimuli can only solve some problems and make possible the formation of concepts under certain conditions, and that other problems and other concepts require a different mechanism, we can set about to determine the limiting conditions of the two different processes."

Sargent had subjects solve dissarranged word problems. There were three levels of difficulty. "All subjects typically used a 'whole approach' for the first few seconds, then, if an 'immediate reorganization' did not occur, they turned to a 'part approach.' "

The operation of imagination is seen in Ogden's description of reasoning. "At first it builds crude ideas, representations with ill-defined contours and uncertain articulateness, more or less amorphous figures of mind composed of imagery and feeling which initiate and control certain directions of behavior. But as the contour and internal structure of these figures are defined, they become concepts, the members of which are logically ordered."

"One of the functions of imagination is the seeing of things in many different and unexpected relations—an essential factor in all those operations characterized as exhibiting originality or creativeness," says Hartmann. "Integration is the most conspicuous mental process occurring during creation; it alone accounts for the basic theme, and the endless variety of novel forms which emerge can only be explained by this principle. Integration itself depends largely upon certain structural resemblances and similarities between the experiences that it unifies."

Rossman points out that according to the Gestalt theory every act of invention is the completion of a pattern or configuration, which was previously recognized as being incomplete. Likewise, Koffka says, "The perception of a problem situation sets up certain psychophysical stresses in an organism. Thinking is the process by which these stresses are resolved. This process does not involve the present and its immediately engendered tensions alone; it works in conjunction with and through the trace column, the masses of traces, ultimately of a chemical nature, left by past experience."

"New combinations are obviously not simply accumulations, but rather completions of structures," in Duncker's description. "Elements are set in relations. Each 'application' of general statements, general experiences to new material occurs through structural combination. Of course, it is not the traces themselves which participate in such a combination, but rather actual processes which are 'derived' from the former.

"The general law of structural combinations runs as follows: Excitations of any two traces, ideas, or images, or of an idea and a percept, may actually be put into any relation whatever into which (according to their nature) they can enter as related terms. Combinations can be conditioned from within (compare the free play of imagination) as well as determined from without (verbally). Whoever reads a novel, carries out from the first to the last page verbally determined combinations. Incidentally, combination is nothing but a special case of 'restructuration of material' in general."

Wertheimer indicates the differences between his theory

of the course of thinking and associationism. He says that the thinking process is direct and productive. The central processes are found in grouping, in centering and reorganization. The features and operations are related to a whole and are dynamic and structural. The processes are not and-summative aggregations, not arbitrary or fortuitous, but show a consistency in development.

Creative imagination is "an acquired personal possession, structured out of experiences and strivings, a living system which has undergone a developmental organization and is still actively growing," according to Gesell. This is true of scientific as of artistic imagination. Creative imagination is "a dynamic system which grows with what it feeds on, sets up new tensions leading to new patterns. Some of the patterns may have an element of surprise and of dramatic discovery, but the basic gains are increments of gradual growth."

Lewin states that bonds between mental events are not the motors of future mental events. The energizing force which causes one event in a train of thought to follow another is rather the total play of mental forces operative at the present moment, which uses past experience as purely inert material. The connections between events are important, but only as determining the form which mental events will take, not as initiating them.

Imagination Is the Basis of Invention

The importance of imagination in creative work has been stressed by Rossman who says, "Imagination is the basis of invention." Likewise [1]Mach suggests that "abstraction and imaginative activity have the main share in the discovery of 'novel knowledge.'" There is considerable evidence for the view that "only elements of experience are brought into new combinations; the 'original creation' of really new fantasy construction is held impossible," according to Stern. "The

1 Duncker (37)

imaginational onset, which, as 'conception' introduces a new act of creation, is less of a 'vision' than an 'impulse'; a vague consciousness of what is to be produced, combined with a strong activating force."

The significance of imagination has also been emphasized by Murphy. "We have begun to realize that it is characteristic of fantasy to be more creative than is logical thought, in the sense that more cues are woven into the composite texture determined by many needs; in the same way the dreams of the night, starting from a complexity of individual determinants, achieve not simply a bizarre but in many respects, a highly creative end-result."

"Creative thinking is the process of imagination," as stated by Shaffer, Gilmer and Schoen. "Imagination represents therefore the highest type of psychological activity, more complex in its constitution and more significant in its results than are acts of sensing, perceiving, remembering, or reasoning."

The creative process in the arts cannot exist without the imagination in the opinion of Rees. "The artists feel the great importance of the imagination to their art."

"With a vivid imaginative faculty and able technique the artist shapes, colors, distorts and symbolizes his feelings by giving them a semblance of concreteness in art form," writes Portnoy.

"The process of creation arises from the excitement caused by the subject matter, and images play a large part in the awareness of that subject," according to Alexander. "These are not images of the work of art, which are in general only got through actual production." Passive imagination is the "idle play of fancy." "The difference of such passive imagination from the creative sort is the absence of purpose." Morris has said that aesthetic purpose is "simply determinate feeling, which in turn is perception or satisfied imagination."

The role of imagination in art is brought out in the following quotation from Feibleman: "The man with a vivid imagination is one who can call upon mental images of things as they could be (and in his opinion ought to be) by placing together in new contexts and associations the elements of the actual world with which he was already familiar (but dissatisfied). . . . Thus what characterizes the artist, what starts him on his way, is not his possession of an imagination, for everyone has that, but his possession of intense imagination. The artist takes off from experience but so does everyone else, and it is the way in which he uses that experience that characterizes the artist."

When the work of poets and artists is compared with that of persons who lack such abilities, we find more imagination in the former. Patrick, in comparing the poems written by fifty-five poets and fifty-eight non-poets about a picture, notes that the poets have a wider imagination. The poet sees more significance in the scene which is presented to him. He reaches further and tries to link up the concrete scene with something which is universal and fundamental. It is more characteristic of the poets than of the non-poets to look for some deep meaning in the picture—something of emotional value, or something suggestive of human life. Likewise the artists, who drew pictures about a poem which they read, showed wider imagination in their work than non-artists who did the same thing. The pictures drawn by the artists reveal more significance and meaning and possess a unity which is lacking in that of the non-artist. Thus, both of the groups skilled in creative work show greater imagination and a wider range of associations than the two groups who lack those types of ability.

Also in science "autistic thinking may promote imaginative ideas which serve as a meaningful foundation for logical thinking," as Britt suggests. "Scientific experiments in their culmination represent a great deal of logical, objective thinking, but they could scarcely be carried on unless the originator of the investigation at some time engaged in a great deal of autistic thinking or free association of ideas."

Likewise Platt and Baker write that a scientific hunch "springs from a wide knowledge of facts, but is essentially a leap of the imagination, in that it goes beyond a mere necessary conclusion which any reasonable man must draw from the data at hand. It is a process of creative thought." James speaks of the role of imagination which says that what marks off reasoning proper from "mere revery or 'associative sequence' " is the "extrication of the essential aspect out of a given fact."

Phantasy explains the creative force responsible for original discoveries of science and art, according to Elsenhaus. Also, Gordon says that the concrete products of art, science and industry are due to imagination. Gilbert's definition of invention is the sudden and unexpected appearance in consciousness of images juxtaposed into original associations.

Discussion of Imageless Thought

At this point we might consider the question of the occurrence of different kinds of imagery in the imaginative activity of creative thought. Much experimental work has been done in the past in regard to whether or not thinking is carried on by means of images and if images are essential to thinking. Individuals vary in regard to the amount of visual, auditory or kinesthetic imagery which they experience. There is no predominant type of imagery in creative thought as indicated by the results of experiments on the relation of images to other types of thinking. Einstein[1] has written concerning his mechanism of thought: "The psychical entities which seem to serve as elements in thought are certain signs and more or less clear images which can be 'voluntarily' reproduced and combined." Buhler[2] has said that there is abundant evidence of thought without either verbal or vis-

[1] Hadamard (58)   [2] Woodworth (207)

ual images and believed that the thoughts are the essential phenomena in thinking, the images being incidental.

According to Woodworth (1915) "what is imageless is not thought so much as recall. Even the most ordinary facts—the location and style of a building, or the contents of one's pockets—are often recalled without images. Any sort of observed fact is recalled in many cases without the sensory background of the original experience and also, for the first moment, without verbal images.

"With Titchener the problem of imageless thought took a different turn. He wished to make sure whether any new elements of conscious content must be recognized in view of the results of Buhler and others. Already recognized were the elements of sensation and feeling. Was there also a thought element? Was there an independent feeling of relation? His procedure in attacking this question was first to rule out meaning and object reference as not genuine existential content, and second, to see whether his O's reported any genuine content which did not fall under the accepted classes. He and his pupils and his pupils' pupils came to a negative conclusion, since their O's reported (besides meanings) only images, kinesthetic, and organic sensations, and feelings (Clarke, 1911; Comstock, 1921; Crosland, 1921; Gleason, 1919; Jacobson, 1911; Okabe, 1919). They concluded that the reports of imageless thought emanating from other laboratories were due partly to the failure to separate meaning and content, and partly to the difficulty of observing vague images and sensations when one is actively thinking and intent upon meaning. The sensorial content may easily be overlooked, 'so quick is the process of thought and so completely is the attention of the subject likely to be concentrated on meaning. We have a parallel case in the neglect of after-images . . . in everyday experience when other things are in the focus of attention' (Comstock, 1921).

"The supporters of imageless thought were inclined to question the importance of such images as occurred in thinking. Images could occur as associative byplay without furthering the progress of thought. Comstock (1921) held that nearly all the images reported in her experiment had some use in 'anchoring' the problem, carrying the meanings, providing leads for thought, or checking the conclusion. Hollingworth (1911, 1926) made the point that the logical irrelevance of many images need not interfere with their dynamic potency. When the objects that really stand in a certain relation are not easily imaged, substitute objects may take their place. This is the method of symbolic thinking. Words take the place of things, and a spatial diagram or a hand movement does service in thinking of many kinds of relation. Hollingworth reported that in his experience 'present kinesthetic impressions or motor tendencies logically irrelevant are most frequently the vehicle or garment which plays the substantive role in relational consciousness.' "

Woodworth concludes that "tactual, kinesthetic and other sensations must always be present, and in the full sense there are therefore no moments of experience deprived of all sensory content. That visual or verbal images are usually present is also probable, except indeed when one is attentively looking or listening. The important question is whether at the dawning of a thought the meaning comes first . . . or the words or other symbolic and illustrative images. Even this question is not so important, the real question being whether meanings are present. If meanings are ruled out as non-existent and non-occurrent, then no imageless thoughts will be found, for the imageless thoughts are simply the meanings which the O's report with such ease and certainty.

"It is curious what different semi-emotional reactions are made by different persons to the notion of imageless thought. To some it seems entirely natural and acceptable, while others shrink from it as a strange, mystical theory and insist that there simply must be some image or sensation to 'carry the meaning.' Since superfine introspection would be needed to establish the complete absence of all imagery at a moment of active thought, the whole question may well be shelved as permanently debatable and insoluble." Woodworth concludes that "imageless thought is no more mysterious than the everyday perception of facts."

As yet no definite relation has been established between the predominance of a certain type of imagery and the consistent use of a certain type of medium to express the results of creative thought. For instance, no measures have been obtained to show the relative proportions of visual, auditory and kinesthetic imagery in the mind of a poet writing a poem as compared with an artist painting a picture or a musician composing a symphony. No doubt, there is large individual variation even among persons working in the same medium.

Reverie and Phantasy of Average and Psychotic Persons

In the fast tempo of our modern life it is unfortunate that psychotic persons are about the only ones who spend a lot of time in imaginative thinking. The psychopath is one who has been faced with a problem which is too difficult for him to solve. He has plenty of leisure for creative thinking, because he no longer permits the demands of usual, everyday living to interfere with his thoughts. Creative thinking appears with them because the two important conditions have been fulfilled, namely, they are faced with problems too difficult for them to solve and they have plenty of leisure in which to think. As a result, the psychopathic individual is one who has passed through the first three stages of creative thinking.

In the reveries of the average person and the phantasies and daydreams of the psychopath, as well as in productive creative thought, an unsatisfied want underlies the process. In each case the person is faced with a difficult problem. During the prolonged unpleasant stage of preparation the thinker is distressed. His repeated unsuccessful attempts are accompanied by a rising sense of failure. He feels thwarted and depressed. Likewise, the stage of incubation in which certain ideas recur from time to time is often unpleasant. Even when he is engaged in other activities he keeps thinking about the problem in spite of himself.

In the case of the psychotic the period of conflict and distress has been unduly prolonged and intense. The person has worried about his problems a great deal. His lack of success and repeated failures have aggravated his unhappiness.

Then suddenly in the stage of illumination he arrives at an idea for a solution. He experiences keen joy and elation at having found an answer to his baffling problem. All the unhappiness and distress of the preceding stages is superseded by great happiness. His elation is even more pronounced because of his previous prolonged conflict and distress.

The psychopathic person clings to this idea which has brought him such happiness. He cannot bring himself to face the unpleasantness of revising and checking it against reality in the final stage of revision or verification. He shrinks away from the laborious and highly distasteful task of criticism, which would be necessary if he modified his solution to conform to reality. Instead he spends hours dreaming about this idea, which brings him so much pleasure, and elaborating it. Sometimes the patient's elaboration of his false idea leads him to thoughts which make him unhappy, as in types of psychosis characterized by depression.

In the reverie of the average person, on the other hand, the pleasant idea may soon be forgotten, because of the duties of daily routine, without being carried to the final stage of revision or verification. He does not cling to it as the psychopathic person, who has been distressed by prolonged conflict. Frequently, however, the reveries of the average person are finally checked with reality in the final stage of revision or verification and may result in the creation of a work of art, an invention, or a scientific discovery.

The ordinary person has the courage to face the unpleasantness inherent in the revision and verification of the pleasing idea obtained in illumination. He is willing to put forth the effort to accomplish the disagreeable task of testing, changing, or elaborating the idea obtained in illumination, according to the standards of art, science, or everyday living. The psychotic .person, on the other hand, shrinks from the unpleasant or disagreeable contact with reality, which would be forced upon him in the revision or verification of his cherished solution. Instead he clings to his cherished idea and shrinks from the external world because it is unpleasant.

If the psychotic person can reach the point where he can critically evaluate his cherished ideas to some extent, he is on the road to recovery. When treatment by any of the methods of therapy enables a psychopathic person to modify and criticize his cherished daydreams in contact with reality, his creative thinking, instead of being absurd or peculiar, will produce results in conformity with the facts of the external world, just as the average person's does. When the psychotic person can be induced to think along those lines, he will be able to function again as an average individual in society. If psychotic creative thinking can be induced to pass into the final stage of verification or revision, it will be brought into correspondence with the facts of the external world, as the average person's creative thought is done.

Summary

Imagination has been described by various writers as the fusion of images or elements of past experience into new combinations. Other descriptions emphasize the importance of cues in redintegration, the factor of the whole complex, or the eduction of relations. Pattern or configuration is prominent in the Gestalt presentation. Since sensations and images are usually present it would be difficult to ascertain the complete absence of all imagery at a moment of active thought. Imagination is the basis of invention, art, or scientific discovery. Imaginative activity in reverie or psychopathic day-dreaming is differentiated from creative thought by the absence of the final stage of verification, in which the idea obtained in illumination is evaluated in accordance with the objective facts of reality. When any of the methods of therapy induces the creative thinking of the psychotic to pass into the final stage of revision or verification, it will be brought into correspondence with the facts of the external world like the average person's creative thought. But before any psychological method is used the physical condition of the nerve cells should first be restored by the use of the proper chemicals.

8

RELATION OF THE LOGICAL STEPS OF REASON-
ING TO THE PSYCHOLOGICAL STAGES

CREATIVE thought and reasoning have been variously
described by different investigators. Both the psychological stages and the logical steps of reasoning have been
discussed.

Logical Divisions

In describing the latter, Dewey writes that "a complete
act of thought has five more or less logically distinct steps:
(a) a felt difficulty, (b) its location and definition, (c) the
suggestion of a possible solution, (d) the development by
reasoning of the bearings of the suggestion, (e) further observation and experiment leading to acceptance or rejection." First a problem, perplexity or difficulty arises. The
next step is the observation or recall of significant facts
about the problem. In the third step an hypothesis is suggested as a possible solution. In the fourth step the implications of the hypothesis are developed and it is subjected to
criticism. In the final stage the solution is verified by concrete application or further reasoning.

In a similar manner Burtt describes five steps of reflective thinking as:

(1) Occurrence of something felt as a perplexity

(2) Observation designed to make clear precisely what the difficulty is

(3) Occurrence to mind of suggested solutions of the difficulty

(4) Reasoning out the consequences involved in the suggestions thus entertained, and evaluating the suggestions by their aid
   a. deducing the consequences of suggestions
   b. comparing them as thus expanded in the light of the controlling problem
   c. selecting the most promising suggestion

(5) Observation or experiment to test by empirical fact the suggested solutions in the light of their implications

(6) In some cases of reflection there may follow what is temporarily a sixth step, consisting in a survey of the preceding thinking to uncover any inadequacies that might be corrected.

The difference between steps one and two is the difference between vaguely feeling that one is in a difficulty and formulating conditions which must be met. Steps two and three sometimes seem to merge, but they are really very different. "Step three is a rise in the mind of possible solutions of the problem, step four, a reasoning process in which the consequences bound up with these suggested solutions are traced." The dividing line between steps four and five is the line between thinking out what ought to be a present fact, if such and such be the case, and looking to see whether it is a present fact or not. Burtt says some problems "deal so entirely with relations of ideas that no action subsequent to the fourth step seems to be needed," as for example, pure mathematics. In other problems the "action entered upon is a part of the reflective act itself, which accordingly requires a fifth step. These comprise some practical problems and all the problems in which we are trying to understand some fact or facts susceptible of observation by the senses," as for example, in the sciences except pure mathematics.

Likewise Billings asserts, "The formal steps in reasoning, as found in the literature, are: a problem; an understanding of the problem, or judgment; the solution of the problem or inference; a conclusion; a belief in the conclusion; verification; proof; and application. From the psychological point of view, the last three are not parts of the real reasoning process; but are follow-up processes for the purpose of testing or checking up on the conclusion, which really ends the reasoning process. Verification is but supplementary proof; application is but practical proof; and induction and deduction are the logician's method of proof. . . . Thus, we may conclude that the essentials of reasoning may be reduced to a problem, an understanding of the problem, and the solution of the problem, which presupposes essential experiences and ability."

According to Symonds there are five steps in making a decision. These are: first step, isolate values involved; second step, judge and select between the values; third step, discover facts with regard to the situation; fourth step, estimate consequences of various alternatives in the light of values set up; fifth step, weigh relative strengths of satisfactions, dissatisfactions, comforts, pleasures, annoyances.

Mossman also points out the logical steps by which an individual solves a difficult problem: "(1) he asks to know all the factors which he can locate and which he thinks are necessary to his meeting the situation. In considering these factors, (2) he takes account of their value for him, what he thinks they are worth in his attempt to deal with the situation; (3) he formulates a plan of action; (4) he accepts the plan as his way of meeting the situation and decides to act in accordance with it; (5) he acts upon this, the result of his own thinking; (6) he accepts the consequences and assumes the responsibility for what he does. In so doing, he contrives and accepts, as his, a way of behaving in meeting this situation. . . . These steps are applicable to any new situation, be it the solving of a geometry problem, the making of a necessary decision, the painting of a picture, the composing of a ballad."

Instead of describing the process of reasoning in terms of five or six logical steps, Feibleman has emphasized four main divisions. He writes, "In the psychology of artistic expression, logical form exists as a kind of structural framework. For the making of a work of art there are (a) premises (b) method (c) applications (d) conclusion. (a) The premises of a work of art are those ideas or feelings or both which the artist decides he wishes to express. . . . Once the premises are chosen the artist is to that extent no longer free; he can not arbitrarily do whatever he wanted to do but only what the premises allow him to do; he has by accepting them set up his own restrictive conditions. . . . (b) The adoption of a method of artistic expression is part of the acceptance of premises. Although absolutely essential, in that there can be no work of art without some method, the method is a kind of secondary premise; for what is to be done takes logical as well as temporal precedence over *how* it is to be done, and the selection of premises must follow this order. . . . (c) The applications of the premises according to the method consist in the actual steps taken to produce the work of art. These may be . . . any specific procedures involving physical action and intended to produce an independent and public product. This is the part of the process which may be viewed objectively. An artist seen at work is generally an artist engaged on this stage of his project. . . . (d) The conclusion of the artistic process consists in the finished work of art together with its meaning. When the last application has been made, the work of art stands completed, a whole thing, destined perhaps to lead a life of its own in the social world."

Blanshard has described three logical divisions in the process of reasoning. The steps in the process of reflection are: (1) to specify the problem and make it definite; (2) to read and consult until one gets the material for a suggestion; (3) the leap of suggestion.

Psychological Divisions

Other writers have stressed the psychological more than the logical divisions in the process of thought. Christof writes that three distinct stages in the total course of thinking are: (1) formulation of problem, (2) elaboration (3) solution. The formulation of the problem is marked by bafflement and the search for the significance of an obscure and puzzling situation which often includes imagination or other easier substitutes for real thinking. When formulation has been effected, a general procedure for reaching a solution is developed. In elaboration there are three moments: (a) accumulation of psychological products in which food for thought is assembled; (b) valuation and selection in terms of the relevance to the task with many reversals, revivals, and reconstruction; (c) fusion and synthesis of the selected products. Although the three moments in elaboration are not always temporarily distinct, the fusional and integrational phase is logically last. The solution of the problem derives from elaboration. The final step may give only partial solutions or end in defeat. Bentley also speaks of these three stages. In solution, the final product appears in various forms of discovery, decision, doubt, affirmation, and rejection, or in a revised formulation of the original task.

Ribot had previously divided creative thought into three phases. He speaks of two processes in creative thought, the complete process and the abridged process. In the complete process there is the first phase, the idea (commencement) with special incubation of more or less duration. The second phase is invention or discovery. The third phase consists of verification or application. In the abridged process, the first phase consists of general preparation (unconscious). The second phase consists of the idea, inspiration, eruption.

The third phase is the constructive and developing period. "The two processes differ superficially rather than essentially." In the complete process the first phase is long and labored (preparation); in the abridged it is negligible. In both the complete and abridged the second phase is the same: it lasts only an instant. In both processes the third phase may be long or short because the main work is done.

We find that Luzzatto distinguishes three moments, as he calls them, in artistic creation. The first is the simplification of reality in the active enjoyment of a natural spectacle or manifestation of human life. This moment is not specifically an attribute of artists, but belongs to all who possess a spontaneous sensibility. The second moment of creation is typical of the artist; it is the moment when the simplification is transformed into communicable form. The third moment is that of execution.

Likewise Portnoy asserts that there are three stages of creative thought. In the initial phase the artist is quiet or frenzied. In the second stage the "artist feels less apprehensive, he once more anticipates a feeling to write, paint or compose. It is a transitional stage during which the artist confines himself to routine matters of cleaning brushes, filling in detailed parts of an orchestration, rewriting old manuscripts." The third stage "follows finding the artist in his glory. Ideas flow, the eye sees, the ear hears, the artist is keenly alive again. He works with abundant energy until exhausted."

Two main stages in reasoning have been pointed out by James. "First, sagacity, or the ability to discover what part, M, lies embedded in the whole subject which is before him; second, learning or the ability to recall promptly M's consequences, concomitants, or implications." Sagacity is necessary to enable us to "extract characters—not any characters, but the right characters for our conclusions." Heidbreder studied concepts obtained from various categories of stimuli.

Moreover Duncker writes that "the whole solution-process may be divided into two stages: 1. The stage of explications (of the goal and especially of the premises) which should lead to the decisive ground—consequence relation, and must therefore themselves occur relatively at random. 2. The stage in which the decisive relation 'snaps into place,' with all the 'completions' it makes necessary." In regard to the first stage he mentions analysis of conflict, analysis of material, analysis of goal, and solution by resonance. The finding of the solution takes place ultimately through a sort of excitation by equality or resonance.

A description from the Gestalt point of view is also given by Wertheimer, who writes, "Generally speaking, there is first a situation, S1, the situation in which the actual thought process starts, and then, after a number of steps S2, in which the process ends, the problem is solved. Let us consider the nature of situation 1 and situation 2 by comparing them, and let us then consider what goes on between, how and why. Clearly the process is a transition, a change from S1 into S2. S1, as compared with S2, is structurally incomplete, involves a gap or a structural trouble, whereas S2 is in these respects structurally better, the gap is filled adequately, the structural trouble has disappeared; it is sensibly complete as against S1.

"When the problem is realized, S1 contains structural strains and stresses that are resolved in S2. The thesis is that the very character of the steps, of the operations, of the changes between S1 and S2 springs from the nature of the vectors set up in these structural troubles in the direction of helping the situation, of straightening it out structurally. This is quite in contrast to processes in which some steps, some operations coming from various sources and going in various directions, may lead to the solution in a fortuitous, zigzag way." Thus we find that some investigators emphasize three main psychological divisions of productive thinking, while others describe two. Let us see how these descriptions compare with the four stages of preparation, incubation, illumination, and revision or verification. Ribot, for instance, combines preparation and incubation in his "first phase." Christof and Bentley combine illumination and revision or verification in their "third stage of the solution." Luzzatto combines preparation and incubation in his "first moment." Portnoy includes both illumination and revision or verification in his "third stage."

Among those who stress two main psychological divisions, James includes preparation, incubation, and illumination in his "first stage." The description given by Duncker and Wertheimer of the first part of the process corresponds to preparation and incubation, while their description of the last part corresponds to illumination and revision or verification.

Hutchinson, writing of the four stages of preparation, incubation, illumination and verification, asserts that the period of insight is "integrative, restorative, negating the symptoms of neurotic maladjustment engendered by the preceding period. . . . The person steps up to a new level of activity and to new possibilities of reaction." In the fourth stage "the required change in attitude returns the mind from its preoccupation with the cognitive and emotional aspects of the insightful experience to the systematic and logical type of effort with which it started its adventure, thus completing the creative cycle of activity, through passivity and insight, back to activity again. Now, however, a new sense of direction has replaced the first aimless and random efforts."

"Four active stages may be distinguished in the making of a work of art, as far as the psychological aspects of the situation are concerned," according to Feibleman. "These may be described as (a) the reception of the data (b) the revision in the psyche (c) the conscious reaction (d) the making of the object. In the first stage, the reception of data, the mind of the artist is a sensitive mechanism like a photographic plate which receives, enters, stores, and records that part of the external world from which it wishes to receive its sense impressions." In the second stage, revision of the psyche, "the data received by the conscious mind are next turned over to the psyche, or the unconscious, for revision." In the third stage, the conscious reaction, "the act is a sudden one, dynamic, and even frenzied. . . . That 'inspiration' which is held to be the sole and sufficient equipment of the artist by so many laymen, is another name for the immediate perception of new relations and values which takes place on this occasion." The fourth stage, "the actual external and public act of making a work of art follows hard upon the conscious reaction to the perception of new relations in the psyche. There is not much that can be said about this last and final stage in the process."

Comparison of Logical and Psychological Divisions

"It will be remembered that we have observed four stages in the psychological process and also four stages of logical analysis," writes Feibleman. "The question obviously arises of whether the four psychological stages are closely related to the four logical steps. The answer is that to some extent they are related, although the correspondence is not exactly one to one, as we might superficially be led to expect. The best explanation of the relationship will be given by comparing them in detail for points of similarity and difference. The first pair to be compared, then, is 'the reception of the data,' (psychological) and 'the premises' (logical). These are, of course, very close. . . . The second pair to be compared is 'the revision in the psyche' (psychological) and 'the adoption of a method' (logical). . . . The revision in the psyche and the adoption of a method are closely related, though not quite in the same way as the reception of the data was related to the premises. For the revision in the psyche is the emotional turmoil from which the logical definiteness of the adopted method is produced. The third pair to be compared is 'the conscious reaction' (psychologi-

cal) and 'the applications' (logical). The conscious reaction
is what drives the artist to make the applications. . . . Thus
the relationship between conscious reaction and applications is much the same as we found it to be between the revision in the psyche and the adoption of a method; the former is the feeling from which the specific determination
of the latter is produced. The fourth and last pair to be
compared is 'the making of the object' (psychological) and
'the conclusion' (logical). . . . In other words, the psychological processes which go on while the artist is actually occupied with the making of a work of art lead inevitably to
that deduction which we have termed the conclusion. Thus
the relationship between the making of the object and the
conclusion is primarily a consequential one."

Ruch has attempted to compare Dewey's analysis of the
problem solving type of thinking with the four stages of
creative thought. He presents Dewey's five steps slightly
modified, as follows: (1) problem, (2) data, (3) suggested solution, (4) evaluation, (5) the objective test or verification.
Ruch says these are the fundamental steps in problem solving, and continues, "The creative thinking of the artist and
the inventor is much like ordinary problem solving, although its steps are less clean-cut. The introspections of artists give the following steps in creative effort: (1) problem
(2) preparation (3) incubation (4) illumination (5) verification." "Preparation, incubation, and illumination all merge
into each other. They correspond to the acquisition of data
and the evaluation of suggested solutions in ordinary problem solving, except that the artist is attempting to convey a
mood or emotion rather than to establish a logical relation.
The artist works primarily with feelings rather than with
facts."

Ruch says that the problem, which he defines as a distinct recognition of a want, is the first step in both types
of thought. As a matter of fact, the unsatisfied want or need
determines the whole course of creative thought until it is

complete, and is present at every stage until the end. It is therefore misleading to postulate it as the first step in creative thought when it is the underlying process which determines the whole course of creative thought until the very end.

Ruch has not clearly differentiated between the logical description of thought given by Dewey and the psychological description of stages of thought given by Wallas and Patrick. The psychological description of the stages of thought applies equally to artistic and scientific thinking, as well as to practical problems of sufficient difficulty. Likewise, Dewey's logical description of the steps in problem-solving can apply equally to scientific thought and to the mental processes of the poet or artist in creating a work of art. Thus the poet, who wants to write a poem, tries to locate material which would be suitable as subject matter for the poem. He may read other poetry, observe his environment, and otherwise cast about for ideas. As he does so, an idea may recur from time to time with modifications. A suggested solution in the form of a topic for his poem occurs in the stage of illumination. The fourth and fifth steps of Dewey's logical reasoning coincide with the last psychological stage of revision. The poet revises the original draft, adding and eliminating words and phrases. Then he compares and checks his poem objectively with the standards of good poetry, as he knows them, and may be forced to make additional revisions and changes until it is completed.

Thus in poetry, art, literature, music, and drama Dewey's analysis of steps in problem solving applies equally well, as in scientific thought.

The logical analysis of steps of reasoning does not take into account the question of the need of rest before illumination or the time order of the different psychological stages. It does not take account of the recurrence of the idea with modifications during incubation nor of the emotional reaction of surprise and elation typical of illumination. The logical description does not show the progressive stages of the mental process which underlies the production of those logical relationships.

The five logical steps of reasoning, as propounded by Dewey, may all appear in one stage, as in preparation, or may extend over the whole of the creative process, if the problem is sufficiently difficult. For instance, the thinker may have a felt difficulty and try to locate and define it. A solution is suggested from his past experience and he reasons out the bearings of the suggestion. He checks the solution against known facts and tries it out in action. All of these five steps may occur in the stage of preparation, and the thinking process is terminated at that point. This is the case in simple problems. The first solution, which occurs to the subject as being probable, is found by observation to check with the facts, and action immediately follows, which verifies the solution. For instance, in a practical problem as trying to determine why a door won't shut, a person examines the characteristics of the door, as its hinges and construction, and the solution is suggested that the casing might be warped, which fits in with the fact that it has been exposed to dampness. Verification is the overt examination of the door for a part of the casing which might be warped, and removing the obstacle.

As pointed out above, in simple problems the five steps of logical reasoning as propounded by Dewey may appear all in the stage of preparation and terminate the thinking process at that point. In difficult problems, on the other hand, the five logical steps of reasoning may coincide with the whole process of creative thought, including the four psychological stages of preparation, incubation, illumination and revision. For instance, in making an invention the inventor during the stage of preparation is aware of the "felt difficulty" and tries to locate it and define it. This may be a complicated and extensive process involving reading, observation, communication with others, and drawing on his own experience. He may work only at intervals and lay the problem aside at times. An idea is apt to start recurring from time to time, often while he is doing matters unrelated to the problem at hand. As it recurs it is modified. The third logical step of getting the solution occurs in the stage of illumination. This is frequently accompanied by affective feelings of pleasure and surprise. In the final psychological stage of revision or verification the fourth and fifth steps of the logical description appear. The thinker reasons out the implications of the invention and then submits it to objective test and experiment.

Summary

In describing the process of productive thinking some writers have stressed the logical steps, while others have been more concerned with the psychological stages. Dewey has formulated five logical steps consisting of a felt difficulty, its location and definition, the suggestion of a possible solution, the development by reasoning of the bearings of the suggestion, and further observation. Burtt, Billings, Symonds, Blanshard, and Mossman have given more or less similar descriptions. The psychological stages have been emphasized by Ribot, James, Luzzatto, Portnoy, Christof, Duncker, Hutchinson, Feibleman and others. In simple problems the five logical steps may all occur in the first stage of preparation and the thinking is terminated at that point. The first solution, which occurs to the subject as being probable, is found by observation to check with the facts. In more difficult problems, on the other hand, the five logical steps may coincide with the whole process of creative thought, including the four stages of preparation, incubation, illumination, and verification or revision.

9

AGE OF PRODUCTIVITY

Age of Peak of Productivity of Best Work

AT what age in the lifetime of a genius does his best creative work appear? This is an important question to be answered in a study of creative thought.

Lehman has studied the various fields of human endeavor to get information on this point. From six age curves based on highly selected bibliographies the maximum productivity of literary masterpieces was thirty-seven years; for eight other curves of ages the peak was at forty-two. The best short stories are most often written at thirty-five years and the best poems between twenty-five and thirty years. "These data make it seem highly probable that the best books have been written most frequently by authors still in their thirties," although good work may be done after that.

Lehman has shown that the peak of the composition of the best instrumental selections lies between twenty-five and thirty years, near thirty; the peak for the best symphonies, chamber music, and vocal solos is between thirty and thirty-five years; the peak for the best grand opera and orchestral music is between thirty-five and forty years, and the peak for the best light operas and cantatas lies between forty and forty-five years. He writes, "It seems likely that both today and in former days, the peak for quality of musical composition appears at earlier age levels than does the peak for quantity of composition."

"The assembled evidence seems to reveal that on the whole a given artist's best oil paintings are more likely to be executed when the artist is from ages thirty-two to thirty-six inclusive, than during any other age interval of equal length. . . . An isolated instance of an artist who has executed his most notable oil painting at any particular age level demonstrates not the probability but only the possibility that such an event may occur. . . . Similarly the age curves that have been presented in the present study demonstrate not the certainty, but merely the statistical probability that a given artist's greatest oil paintings will be executed while the artist is still in his thirties. . . . Therefore, one is justified only in saying that an artist's one best painting is somewhat more likely to be executed from ages thirty-two to thirty-six than during any other five-year interval."

Lehman shows that the best paintings are most frequently produced between thirty-two and thirty-six years of age; the best etchings between thirty and thirty-four years; although for architecture the peak is between forty and forty-four years. "It seems reasonable to conclude, therefore, that in the field of painting, the quality of production falls off at an earlier age level than does the quantity of production." The work of a genius in his old age may still be far superior to the best work which the average man does in his prime. Therefore the comparison is not to be made between a genius and the average man, but between the youth and age of the same genius.

In the movies the peak of the best individual performances is between twenty-three and twenty-seven years for the women and between thirty and thirty-four years for the men. The public demands young women, but the men need not be so young. For movie directors the peak of the best years is between thirty-five and thirty-nine years.

He has also studied the age at which the most creative work is done in each field of science. He shows that the best contributions for chemistry and physics most frequently occur about thirty years of age; and the same is true of mathematics. In astronomy the best achievements occur most often around forty-five years of age. Inventions of the best quality are most frequently made between thirty and thirty-five years of age. In other fields of science Lehman has shown that the peak for the best achievements in bacteriology is thirty-five to thirty-nine years; for physiology, thirty-five to thirty-nine years; for goitre research, thirty-five to thirty-nine years; for pathology, thirty-five to thirty-nine years; for anatomy, thirty-five to thirty-nine years; for medical discoveries, thirty-five to thirty-nine years; for surgery, thirty-five to thirty-nine years; for disease symptoms, thirty-five to thirty-nine years; for drugs, thirty to thirty-five years; for psychology, thirty-five to thirty-nine years; for hygiene, thirty-five to thirty-nine years. In these fields of science "the peak of productivity occurs at ages thirty-five to thirty-nine, inclusive." He concludes that the data do "not support the thesis that men cease to make useful contributions at any specific chronological age level. On the contrary, these data suggest that it is possible for individuals to think creatively and to make invaluable contributions at practically every chronological age level beyond early youth. . . . In medicine and allied fields creative thinking does not cease at forty years or even at sixty years."

Lehman found that "the philosopher's one best philosophical treatise is more likely to be written or just published at ages thirty-five to thirty-nine years than any other five-year interval." This is true for logicians, ethics writers, esthetic writers and general philosophical writers. For social philosophers the interval was from thirty-five to forty-four years, and for metaphysicians from forty to forty-nine years. "The average output of the superior philosophical works is almost as great at ages thirty to thirty-four, as at ages thirty-five to thirty-nine. . . . The peak of an age curve which presents data for philosophical works of the highest merit is likely to be somewhat narrow or pointed, and to occur at not later than ages thirty-five to thirty-nine."

From a study of financial, political, and military leaders Lehman found that the peak of their best work is apt to occur later in life. When account is taken of the fact that more die young, then ages sixty to sixty-four have more large incomes in proportion to its numerical strength. That group "most frequently receives 'earned' annual incomes of $50,000.00 or above, although the absolute number is the largest at ages fifty to fifty-four." In business, "the age group fifty-five to fifty-nine years actually contributes more top-flight (nominal) managers than any other age group, but in proportion to numerical strength, the age group sixty-five to sixty-nine has the largest contribution." The ages of trustees of great American foundations and trustees of American community trust funds show the peak of the curve at fifty to fifty-nine years. "Authority, prestige, and responsibility in American affairs tend to be vested in (or gravitate to) middle-aged men." In regard to two hundred ninety-two incomes of one million or more in 1915–20, a study reveals that the peak of the curve for the absolute number was between sixty and sixty-nine years, but in proportion to its numerical strength the peak of the curve is between eighty and eighty-nine years.

Lehman studied the ages in which appear the peaks for political leadership, as follows: presidential candidates (both successful and unsuccessful), fifty-five to fifty-nine years; governors, forty-three to forty-nine; justices of U.S. Supreme Court (when appointed), fifty-five to fifty-nine years; members of president's cabinet (when appointed) fifty to fifty-four years; presidents of republics other than U.S., fifty-five to fifty-nine years; members of British cabinet, fifty-five to fifty-nine years; chief ministers and prime ministers of England, fifty-five to fifty-nine; and U.S. ambassadors, fifty-five to fifty-nine years. In military fields, the peak of the best work for military leaders is forty to forty-four years; for naval leaders, fifty-five to fifty-nine years.

A study of presidents of over fifty national scientific and learned societies reveals the peak falls between fifty and fifty-five years. "It was found, however, that professional recognition and leadership are won much more quickly in some lines of endeavor than in others. Past presidents of both the American Medical Association and the American Bar Association were found to have held their presidencies most often at ages sixty to sixty-four, inclusive. . . . But for both the American Chemical Society and the American Psychological Association past presidents have served most frequently from ages forty-five to forty-nine." The peak for appointment of presidents of American colleges and universities is between forty and forty-five years.

Lehman asserts that while the peak for military leaders more frequently appears in ages forty to forty-four, top-flight political leaders are most often men of fifty-five to fifty-nine years. A given type of leadership is "due not to any one variable but to an indeterminate number of such factors as self-confidence, forcefulness, persistence, art of persuasion, the ability to grasp and express the will of the masses, the ability to compromise, the times during which a leader lives and so forth." A man attains his peak of physical strength and skill at about twenty-seven or twenty-eight years. "He does not attain his full political stature until approximately thirty years after he has passed the peak of his physical prowess. . . . It has been shown in former articles that several kinds of creative thinking are most likely to culminate when the creative thinker is still in his thirties. But the present study suggests that the top of the political ladder is most likely to be reached by men who are in their late fifties."

In practically all those cases of leadership, when the leader is chosen in recognition of previous achievement, "it would be a logical deduction that the ages of leadership will tend to occur later than the ages of individual achievement." There is a lag between actual achievement and publication, as medical discoveries. "There is almost certain to be a much greater lag between the time of exhibiting the ability to lead and the attainment of eminent leadership, since eminent leadership is likely to result from a general group recognition of the ability to lead. . . . There are, of course, other factors than the lag of recognition behind achievement that prevent youthful leadership. But the slowness with which ability is recognized should forestall the hasty conclusion that the ability to lead necessarily develops when or after eminent leadership has been attained. . . . It seems evident that, when political leadership depends upon something other than the accident of birth into a royal family, the most eminent leaders are most likely to reach to high points in their careers at ages fifty-five to fifty-nine. However, for less outstanding political leaders, the above generalization may not hold true. . . . The earlier ages of state governors than presidents of the U.S. is probably due in part to the fact that a governorship is often a stepping stone to the presidency, many of the presidents having been state governors prior to their election as president."

Lehman has shown that in nearly every field of human endeavor the best productions occur most frequently between thirty and forty years of age. This is true for mathematics, physics, chemistry, biology, medicine, geology, psychology, education, economics, political science, philosophy, most musical compositions, most literary compositions, most types of art and inventions. The peak for poetry is between twenty-five and thirty years and for astronomy, architecture, light opera, and cantatas between forty and forty-five years. Comparing the performances of athletes, composers, painters, authors, mathematicians and philosophers, Lehman concludes, "It seems apparent that the nicest neuromuscular coordination and the best creative thinking must occur (most frequently) at very nearly the same chronological age level. This seeming agreement in such widely different fields . . . seems too good an agreement to be the result of mere coincidence." He writes, "On the whole, our findings suggest that those destined to go far have started early and moved rapidly."

A comparison between the most creative years for workers in each field in past generations and the present generation has been made by Lehman. In physics, geology, mathematics, inventions, botany, pathology, medicine, disease, philosophy, literature, education, economics, political science, public hygiene—all of these types of creative endeavor "the contributions of the more recent era were made at younger age levels. . . . For three of them, namely, chemistry, astronomy, and oil painting no significant age change is evident. Just why 80% of the age-curves which reveal brilliant intellectual attainment should start their descents at earlier age levels for the more recently born individuals, the present writer does not know." Possible causes are: (a) chance factors have probably become less operative with the passage of time; (b) the early amateur investigators were more often self-educated; they had less opportunity to receive formal instruction and to experience the stimulation that is provided by groups of understanding colleagues; (c) the early workers possessed fewer ready-made tools or techniques; (d) during the last few centuries avenues of publication have increased very greatly; (e) prior to the 18th century, mathematicians often withheld their discoveries for prestige; (f) the time-lag between the date of discovery and date of publication may have been decreasing. His data reveal "no factual basis for supposing that the most important creative work of the present day is being done by individuals who are older than the contributors of past centuries have been. Indeed, if any genuine age-change has been occurring (something more than a mere decrease in time-lag) the change seems to favor the younger rather than the older age-groups. And if a review of what has taken place in the past is an indication of what is likely to occur in the immediate future, it seems clear that there is no evidence whatever to support the hypothesis that future generations of creative thinkers will attain their peak output at increasingly older age levels. However, as was stated previously, this generalization does not hold for quantity of output, but only for creative work of the highest merit." But "individual variations at each and every age level are so large and so numerous that careful study of the individual himself should be the court of last appeal."

Farnsworth has made a comparison of eminent musicians of earlier and more recent generations. "We have found the degree of eminence of men in a highly selected list of composers to be unrelated to the length of time since their births or deaths. We have learned that the average birth year of men listed in two contemporary encyclopedias of music occurred much later than did the average of a more highly selected group, and that the average birth year of this latter group came several decades after the average birth year of a still more highly selected group. It would seem, therefore, that the more musicians we rate as eminent the more likelihood there is that we will include in our larger list a greater proportion of composers from the centuries just past."

We have seen that in nearly every line of endeavor the majority of the best work is produced between the ages of thirty and forty years. This is true in those lines of work where individual achievement is the primary factor, but it is not so evident in those occupations where other social conditions are important for success. In other fields, where social factors besides individual achievement are important, the best work is more often produced at later ages, as military leaders in the forties, political leaders in the late fifties, large incomes in the late fifties and sixties. The fact that in almost all the various lines of endeavor, where individual achievement is the important factor, the peak of production of the highest quality is within a narrow age range between thirty and forty years is evidence that creative thought is of the same essential nature in the different fields.

Other writers have pointed out that the best creative work is done at earlier ages. Woodworth has written, "Few great inventions, artistic or practical, have emanated from really old persons, and comparatively few even from the middle-aged." The most productive period is from twenty to fifty years, according to Rossman.

Bjorksten criticizes Lehman's study of the chronological age of intellectual peak performance for having failed to take into account the amount of time available to the scientist for creative work. The pressure of other duties gives the older scientist less time for research. A comparison of the available time against Lehman's curve for output in chemistry shows the two factors to develop and decline quite similarly. The criterion of creative ability, therefore, should not be in terms of absolute output, but rather the ratio of the latter to the number of hours free from such duties he says.

Nelson states that "invention of the very highest order, far from being in decay at forty, seems to be at the very prime or just ready to begin." Adams says the peak of creativity is close to forty-three. He made a list of "4,204 scientists whose ages at the time of their chief work could be determined plausibly from information close at hand." These ages are called primes; the age will mean "the result of subtracting the year of birth from the year in question." His list includes most of the well-known names and many less well-known. The primes before 1600 were not included, otherwise there was no restriction. The median prime of the whole list is forty-three. From the cases of 299 men with early primes, who survived after forty, he notes that research was overwhelmed by teaching, editing, administration of societies, service under government, forsaking science for other fields. "But when all these factors have been considered only a quarter of the early primes can be attributed to them; and the remaining examples of indubitable precocity include many famous names." Adams considers the assertion that scientists take at least the first steps towards their best work before thirty years of age, and concludes, "This plea may or may not be true." He finds that the primes for some of the divisions of science are higher than those of Lehman, as pathology forty-four, surgery forty-five, psychology forty-five, geology forty-six, biology forty-six, engineering forty-three.

We find that Adams' statement that the median prime of 4,000 scientists is forty-three does not accord with Lehman's conclusion that the best creative work most frequently occurs between thirty and forty years for scientists. This discrepancy in results may be due to the fact that he included many less important names in his list. In fact, Adams says that his list includes most of the well-known names and many less well-known. On the other hand, Lehman may have selected his data more carefully when he constructed curves to show in what years the best creative work occurs. Lehman also has presented curves which show that the peak of productivity for creative work of less merit occurs later in life than the peak for work of the highest merit. For instance, he says that the peak for the best contributions in chemistry is thirty to thirty-five years, the peak for the average contributions is forty to forty-five years. "For athletes, for scientists, for the authors of 'best books,' for composers, and for painters in oil, it has been found that the very best work is likely to be accomplished during a narrower age range than is the work of lesser merit." When Adams, in his large sample of 4,000 scientists, included many names of lesser merit, that fact alone would perhaps raise the median of the ages of best creative work for the group. There is need for data to show if average persons also do most of the best work, of which they are capable, between 30 and 40 years of age, or not.

Age of Appearance of Reasoning in Childhood

From this consideration of the age at which creative

thought reaches its highest development, let us now turn to a consideration of how early reasoning first appears in the child.

Piaget made extensive studies of thinking in children. He writes that at seven to eight years argument becomes what it is for the adult—to change from one point of view to the other and to motivate and understand each other. At the age of seven to eight years "we can place the first period of reflection and logical unification, as well as the first attempts to avoid contradiction." A child of eight begins to reflect, reason and understand logical relationships. After that age he becomes conscious of his own operations, and not only of their results, to see if they imply or contradict each other. Similarly, Moore, who gave reasoning problems to about two hundred children, writes, "The power to understand and reject autistic fallacies occurred first in the third grade." At the age of seven to eight, children begin to formulate general principles in words. Grippen writes that creative imagination is seldom found below the five-year level.

Griffiths says the difference between the thinking of the child and the adult, as Piaget shows, is due to the fact that the child's life is more bound round the emotional experiences in which he is submerged and towards which he is unable to adopt an objective attitude. "The result is a difference of emphasis as compared with adult experience. On the other hand, owing to the briefer experience of the child, there is a much lower degree of meaning given to the terms he uses. He copies adult terms but only vaguely understands their meaning." The method which he used in the investigation of imaginative thought or phantasies of children was "one comparable with the clinical method of observation, but supplemented by several 'tests' or imaginative exercises which encouraged the children to express their thoughts freely in speech or action; and enabled them to communicate those day dreams or phantasies which are not ordinarily expressed."

"All the elementary mental mechanisms essential for formal reasoning are present . . ." by the mental age of seven, if not somewhat before. "Development consists primarily in an increase in the extent and variety of subject matter to which those mechanisms can be applied, and in an increase in the precision and elaboration with which those mechanisms can operate. . . . A child's reasoning ability thus appears to be a function of the degree of organic complexity of which his attention is capable. . . . And the development of reasoning appears to consist essentially in an increase in the number, variety, originality and compactness of the relations which his mind can perceive and integrate into a coherent whole," according to Burt. Similarly Glaser states that the elementary mechanisms of thought are present at seven years but are undeveloped.

Constructive imagination usually appears in music at thirteen years, in the plastic arts at fourteen years, in poetry at sixteen years, in mechanical invention at nineteen years, and in scientific imagination at twenty years, according to Ribot. "We know that numbers of men who have left a great name in science, politics, mechanical or industrial invention started out with mediocre efforts in music, painting, especially poetry, drama and fiction. The imaginative impulse did not discover its true direction at the outset; it imitated while trying to invent." Sometimes a person returns to his first creative field. Miller says that the development of the imagination in relation to thinking begins in infancy and reflective thinking occurs at the end of the childhood period.

Other investigators assert that children have the same general patterns of reasoning as adults, but their ability to render explicit all the implications of the concepts they arrive at comes only rather slowly with age. Hazlitt points out that there is "no age limit in relation to the process of thinking beyond that imposed by lack of experience." A further argument against the view "that there is any radical difference between the thought processes of the child and of the adult comes from the fact that when the adult thinks of wholly unfamiliar material he makes the same mistakes as the child." "Piaget's picture of a striking difference between adult and childish thinking is, I believe, due to an over-valuation of verbal expression as a measure of thinking, and an exaggerated view of the logicality of adult thought."

Similarly McAndrew studied children ranging from three to six years of age and concluded that reasoning is possible even with the youngest child. There is a consistent increase with age in the per cent of logical and factual categories. Alpert found that two- to four-year-old children showed insights into problems. Suchodolski states that there "are no qualitative differences between children and adults in logical thinking if problem situations are equated for capacity."

Influence of Some Factors

The fact that creative thinkers produce the greatest number of best contributions in their thirties in nearly all fields of human endeavor, where the individual is not dependent on social recognition for success to a large extent, indicates that the process of creative thinking is essentially the same in all regions of human skill. In those fields where success is dependent on reputation and ability to lead, the best achievement comes later in life, as in military, political and economic leadership. It has been pointed out that the reason the largest amount of best scientific work is produced in the thirties is that as a man attains recognition in the intellectual fields, "he is usually imposed upon by an increasing load of administrative, social, financial, or other noncreative duties." The amount of free time for research is said to decline in both industry and academic work. On the other hand, it is evident that as a man is promoted to higher positions he is more apt to have assistants and clerical help available for working out the time-consuming details of his research. The younger man, on account of his smaller income, often has to spend many hours personally collecting data and working out the details of statistical interpretations by himself. He does not have the funds to hire clerical assistance which is available to the older man. Although the pressure of administrative work may increase, yet the senior creative thinker usually has more assistants and clerical help available if he wishes to do original work.

If the load of administrative duties increases with age for scientists and inventors on the staffs of industrial and academic institutions, is this equally true for artists, writers, and composers, whose peak of productivity for best work is also in the thirties? Many such persons chiefly work alone or spend only a part of their time with institutions.

In our opinion, the pressure of more administrative and financial duties in later life does not explain the general occurrence of the peak of best productivity in the thirties. The fact that in nearly all fields of human endeavor (where individual achievement rather than social recognition is important for success) the peak of best productivity occurs in the thirties, is evidence that creative thinking is the same fundamental process in all types of work.

Effect of Marriage on Creative Thought of Women

Since the peak of best productivity appears in the thirties, perhaps that is an important reason why we do not find the names of as many women as men making the greatest contributions in science and art, for the majority of women are busy raising children at that time. Since this often interferes in the participation in art and science, the women are prevented from working in those fields at the very time when their productivity would be the highest. Hence, even if more women do participate in those fields at older age levels, yet the quality of their work would probably not be as high as if they were working in the early thirties. It is evident that if the majority of women are not engaged in artistic or scientific work at that period, when the human mind reaches the height of its best production, they are not able to develop their greatest abilities in the prime of life.

Is it wise to stifle the creative thinking of women of ability? If superior intelligence is about evenly distributed among men and women, then if a large portion of those individuals are not engaged in creative work at the most productive period of their lives, society has lost much in original contributions to its knowledge and its culture. The advance of civilization is greatly hampered by the lack of favorable opportunities for women of ability to achieve their best creative work.

Facilities to care for children during the day, which are often available for laboring women, should be made equally available for women of superior intelligence and ability. Such facilities would enable society to fully utilize the potential original contributions of a large proportion of its population. Nursery schools, supervised playgrounds, part-time maid service for several families, outside laundry work, and factory production of prepared foods on a larger scale would give women of ability more opportunity for creative work in those years when they are at the peak of their capacity.

Since superior ability is about evenly distributed among men and women, our civilization would have advanced much farther if the potential creative thinking of many women had been utilized instead of stifled. No doubt the appearance of many important inventions has been delayed by this unfortunate situation. When we talk about the expenditure of thousands of dollars for the advancement of science, would it not be well to appropriate a portion of this to establish nurseries, supervised playgrounds and facilities to minimize household duties, so that women of superior ability can make their contributions to our culture? Unless we allow women of ability to develop their capacities to make original contributions, we are hindering the advancement of that same science which we are seeking to promote.

Since many women are attracted to the social sciences, perhaps the world would not be in its present unfortunate condition if society had made use of those vast reservoirs of women's ability in the past. If the number of social scientists had been greater in former generations, perhaps the solutions of some of the most pressing modern problems would have been attained by now. The contributions of only a few scientists of exceptional ability can do much to change the destiny of a country, as the experiments on the atomic bomb have so well demonstrated. For the preservation of society it is necessary to make use of all sources of the best creative work. This can only be done by enabling women of superior ability to combine marriage and a career, and so have the opportunity to produce their finest original work in the late twenties and thirties.

Creative Thinking Essentially the Same In All Areas of Human Knowledge

The fact that in almost all the various lines of endeavor, where individual achievement is the most important factor, the peak of production of the highest quality is within a narrow age range between thirty and forty years is evidence that creative thought is of the same essential nature in the different fields. Spearman says, "Throughout this art as the others, then, the form of mental process essentially involved in creation is everywhere still the same; it is always the transplanting of an old relation, and in consequence the generating of a new correlate." "Heaven-wide apart as are the fine arts and the sciences in some respects, in others they touch each other. Both are composed of precisely the same ultimate elementary processes. . . . And, in particular,

both alike attain their supreme degree of creativity by virtue
of the process which has been called the educing of a 'correlate.' " "The combining imagination joined to the inductive spirit constitutes 'the talent for invention strictly so-
called' in industry, science, artist and poet," according to
Ribot. "Instead of regarding the imagination as a bright but
ineffectual faculty with which in some esoteric fashion poets
and their kind are specially endowed, we recognize the essential oneness of its function and its way with all the creative endeavors through which human brains, with dogged
persistence, strive to discover and realize order in a chaotic
world," writes Lowes. "Yet not more than the lesser are
these larger factors of the creative process . . . the monopoly of poetry. Through their conjunction the imagination
in the field of science, for example, is slowly drawing the
immense confusion of phenomena within the unfolding
conception of an ordered universe. And its operations are
essentially the same."

Similarly Henderson suggests, "Imagination, fantasy,
intuition, discovery by mental lightning flashes, constitute
the supreme creative faculty or faculties of the scientist. The
great scientist shares this god-like quality on equal terms
with the poet, the dramatist, the painter, the sculptor, the
philosopher." "The common heritage of the artist and the
scientist, the consanguinity of the meanings and objectives
of their quest, find verification in their not infrequent ex-
emplification in one and the same person. . . . 'In the vast
orbit in which Leonardo moved, the distinction (between
the artist and the scientist) had little or no existence.' "

Creative imagination is "an acquired personal possession, structured out of experiences and strivings, a living
system which has undergone a developmental organization
and is still actively growing," in Gesell's description. "This
is true of science as well as of artistic imagination." "The
inventor is not unlike the creative artist, but the latter's

work becomes nothing more than an intellectual enterprise when he rules out feeling and imagination," as Portnoy indicates. Hutchinson says that insight is the same in art and science, while Harding asserts, "The principle underlying inspiration in the arts and in science is the same."

The essential similarity of creative thought in the different areas of human endeavor has been stressed by Shaffer, Gilmer and Schoen. "The labor of verification is present in the fine arts as well as in the sciences. The painter must transfer his inspiration to the canvas, and the musician must work out his broad conception in terms of melodies and harmonies. . . . The sciences and the arts judge their creative products by different standards which, in fact, define the distinction between these two areas of creative activity. The scientist's standards for verification are deliberately impersonal. He evaluates his new theory in terms of its agreement with known facts." "The artist, whether painter, musician, or author, has a personal standard of verification. His final task is to *objectify* his inspiration rather than to prove it."

Not only is the process of creative thought essentially the same in all fields, but there is no essential difference in the stages of thought between the creative thinking of the gifted and the non-gifted. Patrick's experiments showed that the same stages appeared in the creative thought of poets and artists and in the thinking of ordinary persons, when they attempted to produce poetry, art, and scientific work.

Although the essential nature of creative thinking is the same for both the gifted and non-gifted, yet there are obvious differences between highly original thought and that of mediocre ability. The poets and artists put more imagination and meaning into their work. They show greater range of ideas than persons who lack those types of ability. The original thinker has a vast reservoir of past experiences on which he can draw in his imaginative activity. The untrained person is unable to discern relationships, which are obvious to the original thinker, and has less skill in the necessary techniques.

Although the four stages appear in all types of creative thought and the process is essentially the same in all lines of endeavor, yet many differences appear in the form and medium of expression. Thus the activity of the thinker during the stage of preparation varies greatly, according to whether he is working in the fields of literature, music, art, chemistry, mathematics, physics, biology, medicine, geology, psychology, law, military science, or finance. The books and articles which he reads, and the material which he collects from his own experience or from talking with others vary greatly in the different divisions of human knowledge. So wide are the differences that a person trained in one field often has great difficulty in comprehending the data of another. Yet in spite of this wide diversity of human training and experience the stage of preparation is essentially the same for each creative thinker.

Likewise the stage of incubation assumes different appearances, according to the discipline in which it appears. The idea which is incubated may be the subject of a poem, the idea for a statue, the theme of a musical piece, a chemical formula, a theory of physics or geology, a mathematical hypothesis, a military plan, or a financial investment. The stage of incubation is evident in all types of creative thought.

The sudden appearance of the correct idea or solution in illumination has been described by various thinkers. Persons working with difficult problems in widely divergent fields have all noted the sudden appearance of the "hunch," whether it be the theme of a play, the subject of a picture, the design for an invention, a law of physics, a medical discovery, a generalization of philosophy or a political plan.

Also the stage of verification or revision is essentially the same in all forms of creative thought. The artist, composer, author, chemist, mathematician, lawyer, sociologist, inventor, economist, or philosopher checks and revises the hunch or solution, which appears in illumination, according to the standards of the discipline in which he is occupied. Although the rules and standards may vary greatly in the different divisions of human knowledge, yet the final stage is essentially the same in each. The creative thinker compares and modifies his idea in accordance with the regulations of the field in which he works.

In spite of the wide variety and diversity characteristic of creative thought, the process is essentially the same in all the divisions of human knowledge. The four stages of preparation, incubation, illumination, and verification or revision appear in all forms of creative thinking.

Whole vs. Part Relationship in Creative Thought

The primacy of the whole over the parts has been emphasized by writers of the Gestalt school. Does this principle also apply to creative thought?

Wheeler asserts that wholes are primary and the parts are derived from them by means of individuation. The whole conditions the activity of the parts, which emerge from the whole "through processes of differentiation and individuation." Also, Ogden says, "Whatever is particularized possesses a cohesive internal structure that implies a membered whole, even though its members cannot be separately discerned." The response to complex stimuli is not the sum of all responses to individual components, but the original pattern in which each part depends upon the organization of the whole, according to Koffka.

Maier describes the process of reasoning by saying that first the thinker has one or no gestalt, then suddenly a new or different gestalt is formed out of the old elements. The sudden appearance of the new gestalt, the solution, is the result of the process of reasoning. Certain elements which one minute are a unity suddenly become an altogether different unity.

"Characteristically the more or less clearly conceived structural whole-qualities of the thing to be created are determining in the process," according to Wertheimer. "A composer does not usually put notes together in order to get some melody; he envisages the character of a melody in statu nascendi and proceeds from above as he tries to concretize it in all its parts. For some composers this is not an easy process; often it takes a long time."

Hutchinson quotes Cyril Burt as saying, " 'Ideas come to me as a whole, usually in verbal form, though I don't know them until I dictate at once either the plan or the rough draft.' "

Meier and McCloy state that the act of reorganizing sense data into a whole requires the ability to recognize clues, form wholes from parts, and perceive relationships.

Patrick studied this question of the logical relationship of the whole to the parts in the creative thinking of poets and artists. During the first two stages, preparation and incubation, the idea, which later becomes expressed in a picture or a poem, does not yet have a definite form. In preparation, ideas often occur without much relation to each other, for they are shifting rapidly. During incubation an idea recurs from time to time, modified as it recurs. This may be either a general idea or mood from the first time that the poet or artist considers making a picture or poem; or it may at first be a small detail which expands into a general idea during the modification which occurs in incubation. The data indicate that either a detail may develop into a general idea, or the general idea may exist from the time that the subject first thought about writing a poem or drawing a picture.

In either case, however, the idea which emerges in illumination is an idea of the whole. The general outline for the picture or the poem appears then. In Patrick's study of scientific thinking the general idea for an experiment as a whole appeared in the illumination stage.

The fourth and last stage of revision or verification consists in developing details. The attention is focused on certain words of a poem or parts of a picture. In scientific thinking the attention is focused on checking various details of an experiment.

The following quotation from a poet reveals how a general idea may exist from the first time he thought about writing a poem: "If I feel blue or excited, then I sit down and try to get it out of my system. Sometimes it grows for days and days, and then I sit down and write it off. The mood comes first and then the phrase." On the other hand, an illustration of a detail which expands into a general idea during the modification, which occurs in incubation, is seen in the following statement from another poet, "I get a word and carry it around in my head. Then other words come. Pretty soon I get a phrase which is the nut of the poem, then I write the poem and modify that phrase."

In either case the primacy of the whole over the parts is apparent in the last two stages, for the general idea in illumination precedes the attention to details in the final stage of revision.

The data obtained from poetic, artistic, and scientific thinking in Patrick's experiments show that in many cases the primacy of the whole over the parts is apparent from the beginning of the process. In other cases, however, the idea of the whole develops from a detail or part during incubation; which idea of the whole in turn precedes the parts or details brought out in revision.

Summary

Lehman and others have shown that in nearly every line of endeavor, where individual achievement is the most important factor, the best creative work is most frequently produced between thirty and forty years of age. But in practically all those cases of leadership, where the leader is chosen in recognition of previous achievements, there is a lag between the time of exhibiting the ability to lead and the attainment of eminent leadership. The elements of formal reasoning first appear about seven or eight years of age, according to some investigators, while others assert that there is no age limit in relation to the process of thinking beyond that imposed by lack of experience. As compared with men, many women are prevented from doing their finest work by family duties in the thirties, when the peak of best productivity is the highest. The fact that in almost all the various lines of endeavor, where individual achievement, rather than social factors, is the most important, the peak of production of the highest quality is within the narrow age range of thirty and forty years is evidence that creative thought is of the same essential nature in the different fields. In many cases of creative thinking the primacy of the whole over the parts is evident from the beginning of the process; in other cases, however, the idea of the whole develops from a detail or part during incubation; which idea of the whole in illumination precedes the parts or details brought out in revision.

10

FAVORABLE CONDITIONS FOR CREATIVE THOUGHT

SINCE we realize that all great discoveries, inventions, and works of art are the results of creative thinking, what can we do to encourage it? How can we stimulate more people to think creatively? How can we improve the quality of the creative work which is being done to-day? In the answer to these questions lies the key to the future of our civilization. Hulbreck states that the cultural trend is against creativeness, despite efforts to help produce it.

Whether our standards of living progress by leaps and bounds, or whether we move forward at a slower pace, depends primarily on the quality of our creative thought. The kind of automobiles in which we shall ride or the type of planes which we shall fly will all depend on the amount and quality of our creative thinking. On it also will depend the laws and sociological reforms, which we will devise to control the destiny of our nation. Likewise, the manner in which we meet the difficult, complicated international problems of the present and the future will depend upon the excellence and extent of the productive thinking of individuals.

The ability to do creative thinking is not only the gift of a few persons. We all have the capacity to do creative thinking to some extent. This has been amply demonstrated

145

in experiments on poetic, artistic, and scientific thinking. When persons without any special training or ability attempted to do creative work, their thought processes showed the same essential stages as the thinking of poets, artists, and scientists. The creative thought of the layman shows the same essential characteristics as that of the famous man of letters. Although wide differences in training, knowledge, and ability appear in the work of the world-renowned thinker and the man of the street, yet the mental processes of both present the same fundamental stages.

Since we are all capable of some sort of creative thought, we next ask ourselves the question, "What shall we do to get better results?" What are the conditions which promote creative thinking? On the other hand, what changes should be made in those circumstances which hinder its appearance? Thurstone suggests study of the nature of thinking that leads to insight and methods to objectively differentiate creative talent.

If we examine many types of creative thinking we become aware of two fundamental conditions for its occurrence: the problem should be sufficiently difficult and the time should not be too strictly limited. In other words, the thinker should have a sense of leisure as he proceeds to solve the problem.

If the time is too short and definitely fixed, the person is apt to recall a solution, which he made in a similar situation in the past, and let it go at that, without trying to solve the problem more accurately. Those situations which have the short, fixed time limits for the response are typically the ones which produce the snap judgment and the snap reply. If the time is too definite, the thinker will give a less suitable solution in order to conform to the prescribed limit rather than seek for a better answer, which he would do if he were able to work with a sense of leisure. A sense of freedom from time restrictions is of primary importance for the development of creative thought.

The other fundamental condition is that the problem must be sufficiently difficult for the thinker. If it is solved too easily, perception, or a short reasoning process, will suffice to give the answer and creative thinking will not develop. However, if a problem is of sufficient complexity, a person will not be able to reach an easy solution at once by memory, perception or a short reasoning process. The difficulty of the problem forces him to think about it from all angles and to keep thinking about it. During the stage of preparation, with its many changing ideas and thoughts, the subject continues to wrestle with his difficult problem. As he does so, an idea reappears from time to time, which is characteristic of incubation. As the idea reappears it is modified, until at last it appears as the solution in the stage of illumination. Since even then the solution is not sufficiently accurate, the final stage of verification or revision is necessary. Hence, one of the chief requisites for the occurrence of creative thinking is that the problem be of sufficient difficulty in relation to the ability of the subject.

Acquisition of Information

Once we realize that we are all capable of creative thought, we naturally ask ourselves the questions, "What can we do to improve the quality of our thinking?" "How can we assist ourselves and others to do more original work?" A number of writers have given beneficial suggestions, which we will now consider.

"One of the best conditions for inventing is an abundance of material, accumulated experience," according to Ribot. "The revelations of inventors or of their biographies leave no doubt as to the necessity of a large number of sketches, trials, preliminary drawings, no matter whether it is a matter of industry, commerce, a machine, a poem, an opera, a picture, a building, a plan of campaign, etc." Accidental discovery usually comes after persistent search, in

Rossman's opinion, and Poincare has said, "These sudden inspirations . . . never happen except after some days of voluntary effort."

If we consider how Coleridge composed his famous poem, *Kubla Kahn,* we find that he had read copiously before writing it. Gesell has pointed out that "genius may have effortless moments which suggest inspiration, but these moments are usually preceded by prolonged periods of preparation. . . . The scientific genius is a prodigious worker, endowed with persevering patience." Portnoy describes artistic creation as "more likely to be 99% perspiration and 1% inspiration, the common notion to the contrary." This is evident in the following quotation from [1]Arnold Bennett: "Today I took up my novel again, and after roughly scribbling 2,300 words in three hours, began actually to have a dim vision of some of the characters—at last. To 'get way on,' there is nothing like seizing the pen and writing something, anything, about one's characters." [2]Liszt describes his study of literature and music as follows: "I study them, meditate on them, devour them with fury; besides this I practise four to five hours of exercises. . . . Ah! provided I don't go mad, you will find an artist in me. Yes, an artist such as you desire, such as is required nowadays!"

Teachers frequently assert that they do not want to teach their students facts, but that they wish to teach them to think for themselves. This is not practical according to Shaffer, Gilmer and Schoen, "for an absence of information has never produced a worthwhile new idea. Admittedly, to cram students with undigested facts alone is undesirable. The slogan, however, should never be 'not facts but thought'; instead it should be 'facts *and* thought.' It also saves time to know the history of one's field of endeavor, so that no effort is wasted in the pursuit of an hypothesis long

[1] Rees (155)   [2] Rees (155)

since disproved. Great thinkers have been scholars, and great artists have been skillful; there is no evidence that originality is ever contaminated by knowledge." Pyle states that one can be trained in reasoning by getting wide experience in his field and being cautious and examining all the facts, as well as by putting his own conclusions to practical tests. A mastery of the technical aspect of the problem is not enough in Harding's opinion. Knowledge outside and beyond one's profession is helpful in promoting original ideas.

"Replies from several hundred research workers and directors of research indicate that certain conditions are definitely favorable to creative mental effort, while others are equally unfavorable," according to Platt and Baker. "The mind must be well provided with facts." Reading similar work, reading opposing work, and talking with two or three people are helpful.

In regard to musical composition Willmann obtained statements from musicians showing their work resulted from conditions, as the study of a poem and consciously getting into its mood; stimulation by the dance, the printed word or abstract sounds of instrumental, orchestral, or vocal music; seeing a painting; contemplating the beauties of nature; or being aroused by some human emotion. Similarly, Bahle asked composers to write songs to poems. The texts, which affected the composers' emotions or had some connections with their former experiences, stimulated them more. The non-musical elements of the poetry seemed to be more important than musical elements in providing ideas for musical compositions.

Harlow points out that the "fact that an individual has previously acquired either habits or organized response patterns that can lead to the effective solution of a particular problem is not, of course, sufficient to insure he will be able to utilize these response patterns when faced with the problem."

Cultural Background

Although an inventor is usually of superior intelligence, history indicates that "many an inventor simply created or discovered some idea which would have been discovered by somebody else if he had not done it." Britt writes, "In other words, if you have a certain interaction of social forces, they will result in an invention by one person or another. The fact that so many inventions have been made by two or more people is an indication of this. . . . No invention is ever made until its elements are present in the existing culture. Every invention is made on the basis of previous inventions. For example, the automobile could never have been invented (1895) unless there had been a number of other inventions before it, namely, the water jacket (1833), the differential gear (1840), pneumatic rubber tires (1845 and 1883), the electric gap and spark (1860), the compression engine (1876), the clutch and gear (1887), the gas engine (1888), the friction clutch and drive (1891). Without these other inventions, the automobile never would have been possible. The need for it was great long before it was invented, but the cultural basis had not been prepared. The same applies to electricity and to radio and television."

Wide-Awake Attention, Optimism, and Sense of Humor

Another important condition for creative thinking is "a great interest in the problem and a desire for its solution," according to Platt and Baker. The ability to seize upon the chance occurrence and to profit by it has been emphasized by Ribot. "One must first possess the spirit of observation, wide-awake attention that isolates and fixates accident."

"The generalization of curiosity is, however, just as practicable as is the generalization of any other attitude, provided it be not left to chance, but systematically encouraged," according to Murphy. "The struggle of the mind to

keep itself free from every sort of bondage, to remain curious, open, unsatiated in all its relations with Nature, is
ten-fold more difficult than the cultivation of a stable, satis-
fying point of view, but a thousand-fold more precious."

The importance of optimism has been stressed by Boraas. To keep one's interest and "avoid worry and confusion"
are also helpful.

"It is sometimes alleged that a sense of humor and the
spirit of intellectual play are aids to versatility," according
to Carr. ". . . The importance of this mental trait can hardly
be overestimated. It is the basic root of inventiveness and
originality, and it is usually regarded as one of the primal
characteristics of genius."

Flesch suggests "turning the problem upside down," not
being "afraid of the ridiculous," and "knowing the time of
day when your mind works best," to arrange your schedule
accordingly.

Motivation

Motives which promote creative thought have been discussed by Rossman. He cites love of invention, desire to
improve, financial gain and necessity. Bahle suggests that a
composition might be a product of the wishing world of the
composer in that depressing flashes of thought might produce gay melodies and vice versa. An invention requires a
"felt need," according to Britt. There is an old proverb
that "necessity is the mother of invention" but "as to the
first factor, however, 'necessity,' that is a relative matter.
Certainly with the rapidly diminishing supply of gasoline
we now need a less expensive substitute for it; but the necessity has not yet produced a substitute in general use. Certainly men needed railroads and automobiles long before
the present time. The need or necessity was there, yet the
inventions did not come until the cultural period had involved considerable preparation." Horney mentions con-

sistency of interest and effort, the individual's talents, self-confidence, and positive emotional attitude toward work.

Mood and Attitude

When a person engages in creative work his mood is often an important factor. Willmann says that some composers "seem to prepare themselves by getting into the mood of what they want to write. After that they do not spend any conscious effort with the idea and in a day or several days the musical idea appears. This relatively brief working period does not necessarily hold for all composers. . . . There is no special circumstance under which ideas are received by all composers. Neither is there any set working procedure which seems to apply to all of the composers or to any one of the composers all of the time." Benham, who took notes as she wrote compositions herself, observed that "mood set, assuming physical poses and feeling, before composing, definitely affected the composition work and sharpened the results."

All artists, even the most fecund, have experienced an unproductive mood, according to Rees. "James Russell Lowell found that he must wait to write: 'I tried last night to write a little rhyme—but must wait for the moving of the waters.' Cecilia Beaux found too that to save her work she must wait: 'I could not destroy my vision, turn it into leaden, meaningless pigment. I must *wait* for painting.'"

The attitudes which affect thinking have been discussed by Symonds, who writes that "set or fixation is often a hindrance." Such factors as habit, emotion, projection of one's faults on others, and introjection (assuming the good traits of other person for one's self) are influences on thought. "There is the tendency in almost everyone to overestimate the value of his own experiences and to believe as generally true what he has himself observed." Erroneous beliefs are also fostered by the "halo" effect and stereotyped ideas of certain people. Keyes speaks of thinking straight through to the solution of any problem, regardless of its size or source.

Temporary Change from Work on Problem

Frequently a person obtains his most original ideas during periods of rest, half-sleep, light physical exercise, or the pursuit of activities different from those connected with the problem. Helmholtz was aware of the importance of rest for scientific discoveries when he said, "So far as my experience goes, happy suggestions never came to a tired brain nor at the writing table." After fatigue arising from labor has passed away, "there must come a time of bodily freshness and quiet well-being, before the good suggestions would occur." The same thing has been mentioned by Poincare: "Often when a man is working at a difficult question, he accomplishes nothing the first time he sets to work. Then he takes more or less of a rest and sits down again at his table. During the first half hour he still finds nothing, and then all at once the decisive idea presents itself to his mind."

Let us notice a similar suggestion which has been made by Dewey, who has stated: "After prolonged preoccupation with an intellectual topic the mind ceases to function readily.... The mind is ... fed up. This condition is a warning to turn, as far as conscious attention and reflection are concerned, to something else. Then after the mind has ceased to be intent on the problem, and consciousness has relaxed its strain, a period of incubation sets in. Material rearranges itself; facts and principles fall into place; what was confused becomes bright and clear; the mixed up becomes orderly, often to such an extent that the problem is essentially solved."

The importance of rest for getting a "hunch" in scientific thinking has been emphasized by Platt and Baker. After attacking a problem for some time without success, it is often well to abandon it for a time and the solution may suddenly appear. The dangers which lurk are that one may never get an illumination or it is so brief that he fails to grasp it. Likewise Rossman has shown that when an inventor has failed to solve a problem he should lay it aside and the solution is likely to occur at some odd moment when he is not striving for it. Carr has also asserted that baffling problems are sometimes readily solved after an interval of rest. Dimnet recommends that "a prayerful solitude with a dash of austerity in the daily routine is necessary; then, what Tyndall, describing the production of inventions, called 'brooding' and what Newton called 'thinking of it all the time.'"

Voluntary abstention from conscious thought may take two forms according to Wallas. We may do mental work at some other problem or we may relax from all mental work. Maybe a human being gains more from alternation of activity. When a person is baffled "a change of activity, some recreation or relaxation may serve to release the inhibitions against new ideas. Upon a return to the task the persistent errors may have vanished, and a fresh approach can be made," according to Shaffer, Gilmer and Schoen.

The way in which a person may have a "hunch" while he is doing something else, is described by Woodworth, who writes, "About the earliest scientific discovery of which we have any psychological account was that of Archimedes, made during a bath—the original 'eureka' experience—and exactly similar occasions are reported by some of these modern inventors. Others report illumination while riding on a train or automobile, while walking a city street, while dressing, shaving, gardening, fishing, golfing, playing solitaire, listening to a concert or sermon, reading, loafing at one's desk or on the beach, daydreaming, lying in bed after retiring, on awaking in the morning or in the middle of the night." Most of the scientists, whom Fehr investigated, acknowledged the appearance of discoveries while engaged upon subjects foreign to researches at the moment. Weinland asserts that "the time when insight will be achieved is generally unpredictable, although it appears to occur most often while the worker is in a state of mental relaxation, and each individual may find a situation which for him is most predictable."

Periods of Idleness for Autistic Thinking and Relaxation of Routine

We should all realize that periods of idleness, in which autistic thinking may occur, are justified for the promotion of creative thought. Rignano mentions that a state of complete inactivity favors "this entry into activity and fortuitous combination of ideas." The conditions most favorable for inspiration are half-sleep and peace of mind, without sudden interruptions, according to Harding. "Absence of effort, passiveness and receptiveness were shown to be essential conditions. . . . The decisive idea has a way of appearing when the mind is passive and even contemplating nothing in particular." Likewise, Hutchinson asserts that release should be given for free imagination. Periods of idleness are justified. There should be "freedom for growth—autonomy of the creative self." Bohemianism squanders its freedom and returns from hours of dissipation less effective. Creative discipline conserves leisure; it returns refreshed, and invigorated. "The attainment of it (creative freedom) is in fact the hardest part of the creative discipline." Insight often appears during periods characterized by reverie or a slight degree of dissociation.

To relax the pressure of routine is advantageous for creative thinking. Royce points out that a favorable condition for invention is that the subject should vary his own habits, which "are in general useful insofar as they lead towards routine." The individual can vary more when his culture favors individualism.

Murphy also stresses the importance of relaxing routine. He says, "There are latent creative powers which wait to move forward to their work when freed from the restless downward pressures of the alert mind; creative powers which spring into being when once the narrow, nervous, preoccupied world of waking activity steps aside in favor of a quiet integration of all that one has experienced; when one is willing to let the mind leave harbor and travel fearlessly over an ocean of new experience. . . . The historical record of creative thought and the laboratory report of its appearance today are equally clear that creative intelligence can spring from the mind which is not strained to its highest pitch, but is utterly at ease. . . . One aspect of our practical Americanism, our surviving frontiersmen's psychology, with its emphasis on wide-awake alertness and with a touch of Calvinistic devotion to immediate duty, is a suspicion of all these mental states which seem, according to the standard, not to 'get us anywhere'; a general disvaluation of the relaxed, the casual, and the exploratory. The dreamer awakes from an extraordinarily vivid, realistic, intriguing dream, an experience which, if encountered in a novel or a play, he would cherish as a new avenue to the meaning of life. 'A funny dream,' he yawns, and by the time he has his nose in the morning newspaper he has forgotten it. To disvalue the dream is to prove oneself a sensible man. . . . Functional intelligence can be enormously enhanced . . . by the art of withdrawal from the pressures of immediate external tasks, to let the mind work at its own pace and in its own congenial way."

Although alcohol usually reduces attention span and the ability to read and concentrate, Seward and Seward have shown that the ability to draw logical conclusions from syllogisms was scarcely affected at all.

Influence of Professional Reputation and Habits

Often inexperienced persons have an advantage in obtaining original ideas, because their professional reputation is not at stake, according to Rossman. Since they are not hampered by tradition and preconceived theories, they are capable of obtaining a new outlook.

A person's creative thinking may be greatly hindered, because his previously conceived relationships to a given material persist and prevent his viewing the material or situation in terms of new relationships, as indicated by Glaser. Similarly Sells has pointed out that thought is influenced by the "atmosphere effect," which is a "dynamic behavior tendency toward a certain direction or specific type of response." Ruger points out that a person's thinking is hampered if his attitude is that he knows the answer, or if he is interested in himself and how he will act rather than in the problem. The most powerful incentive to a change of attitude is personal success.

Social conventions, as well as conventions of art, hamper the creative movement of the mind according to Fletcher.[1] Pressy suggests that if we shorten the period of education by two years, we lengthen the period of creativity.

Maier asserts that discoveries occur in youth, for people are not hindered by habits then and are better able to get new theories. Men trained in one science often make great contributions in another where they don't have habits already formed. Although learning gives data, it also gives habitual directions and so interferes with new adaptations. The subject is trained to manipulate knowledge. Habitual behavior and persistent directions, which accompany problem solving, may actually prevent solution patterns from appearing.

Opportunities in the Classroom

Certain kinds of school drill and educational methods are detrimental to creative thinking, as Wertheimer emphasizes. "Training in traditional logic is not to be disparaged: it leads to stringency and rigor in each step, it contributes to critical-mindedness; but it does not, in itself,

[1] Rees (155)

seem to give rise to productive thinking. In short, there is the danger of being empty and senseless, though exact; and there is always the difficulty with regard to real productiveness." "There are subjects so educated that they are hampered in their thinking by the habit of proceeding only successively, step by step. But one should not suppose that one always has to do one thing after the other with the idea, 'I'll take care of the other things later.' Try first to see what you are doing in its context, deal with it as part of the context." "I would say that the essential features in genuine solving are: not to be bound, blinded by habits; not merely to repeat slavishly what one has been taught; not to proceed in a mechanized state of mind, in a piecemeal attitude, with piecemeal attention, by piecemeal operations; *but* to look at the situation freely, open-mindedly, viewing the whole, trying to discover, to realize how the problem and the situation are related, trying to penetrate, to realize and to trace out the inner relation between form and task; in the finest cases getting at the roots of the situation, illuminating and making transparent essential structural features of regular series, in spite of the difficulties." "Repetition is useful, but continuous use of mechanical repetition also has harmful effects. It is dangerous because it easily induces habits of sheer mechanized action, blindness, tendencies to perform slavishly instead of thinking, instead of facing a problem freely." "Neither slyness, nor a spirit of domineering, seem to be the most advisable attitude in productive thinking, even though it may sometimes lead to practical success, and thus make for a certain quick, short-range efficiency." There are often strong external factors working against the clean, direct, productive processes as "blind habits, certain kinds of school drill, bias, or special interests."

Various writers have pointed out that it is the function of the school to provide sufficient opportunity for creative thought. Pelikan states, "The drawing lesson has become one of joy and happiness, to which the children look with enthusiasm. The old-fashioned drawing lesson of thirty years ago, where the child copied in a drawing copy book, is as far removed from the present educational methods used, as is the horse and buggy from the modern automobile. Many of these young children have genuine appreciation for form and color, and even for the more modern impressionistic and expressionistic interpretations of our contemporary artists. Unhampered as they are in their outlook on art, and unspoiled as yet by the monotonous repetition of photographic replicas, their efforts are akin to the beautiful work of primitive peoples with whom a certain amount of crudeness is overshadowed by a wholesome sense of design and spontaneity of expression." Florence Cane asserts that "the whole psychological condition necessary for assisting creation presupposes a conscious teacher, educated physically, emotionally, and mentally; one who is supple of body, tender of heart, and adventurous of mind." Guilford speaks of the problem of discovering creative promise in children and promoting the development of creative personalities.

In school imaginative thinking is helped by bringing out the importance of it and by developing an interest in it, according to Boraas. Parker suggests that pupils can be stimulated by defining the problem; recalling related ideas by analyzing the situation and making hypotheses; evaluating each suggestion by keeping an unbiased attitude till the end, criticizing each suggestion and rejecting and selecting solutions systematically and verifying solutions; and organizing material to aid thinking by taking stock from time to time, using methods of tabulation and graphic expression, and expressing concisely tentative conclusions reached from time to time during inquiry. Similarly, Glaser points out that training in abstracting, analyzing, outlining, summarizing and generalizing have been found effective for improving reasoning ability.

Duncker recommends that in teaching mathematics instruction should proceed organically. "In teaching, it is advisable—be it even at the cost of brevity and 'elegance'—to proceed as organically as is feasible, to undertake as few fortuitous explications of premises as possible." Likewise, Wertheimer says, "The attitudes one has developed in dealing with problem-situations—having had the experience of achievement or only of failure, the attitude of looking for the objective structural requirements of a situation, feeling its needs, not proceeding willfully but as the situation demands, facing the issues freely, going ahead with confidence and courage—all these are characteristics of real behavior, growing or withering in the experience of life."

Hartmann writes, "Since all human creations are types of solutions to definite problems, any improvement in the capacity of school children to solve problems on their level may be construed as contributing something to their eventual powers of creation in larger and maturer fields. . . . One of the dangers of ordinary schooling is that it is so successful in discharging part of its task in establishing behavior norms that the maintenance of the plasticity required to transcend them on certain occasions is often impaired. . . . Classroom discussions and programs which repeatedly raise the question, 'Could it be done better and how?' are serviceable in creating an intellectual atmosphere, in which original ideas may flourish. . . . It is regrettable that the hurried tempo of modern life, affecting as it does the school program which is too crowded to do all that is expected, is so inhospitable to the old-fashioned exercises of meditation and contemplation. A daily schedule that cannot find some time for this function of solitary absorption and reshaping of one's miscellaneous information, skills, and aims is an effective barrier to the emergence of many rewarding intuitions. It can be confused with a lazy introspective form of vegetation or with futile daydreaming, yet it is doubtful if any better method of getting the ground ready for creative performances can be devised. . . . Teachers can develop the creative possibilities of their pupils by frequently arranging for productions in miniature planned and executed by the learners themselves. . . . Educational psychology alone cannot supply the proper standards for appraising any novel accomplishment, but it can do much to reduce the fears of teachers and pupils that their creative functions are absent or negligible by acquainting them with the conditions under which they flourish. Original production is an area of human experience from which few, if any, persons are permanently debarred. . . . Psychologists looking over the educational scene at all levels, but particularly focusing their gaze upon the principal stretch of the school system between the kindergarten and the graduate school, have grown more and more convinced that the processes of 'acquisition, impression, intake, and learning' have tended to dominate over those concerned with 'production, expression, output, and creation.' "

Weisskopf states we suffocate intellectual activity by exhorting students to adopt a critical, controlled attitude and regular study habits. Of the four stages of the creative process, preparation, incubation, illumination, and verification, educators "customarily stress the first and last, and ignore the two other important stages."

11

A PROGRAM TO IMPROVE CREATIVE THINK-
ING IN OURSELVES AND OTHERS

IN the preceding chapters we have discussed the nature and characteristics of creative thought. Now we conclude by formulating a program to improve our own thinking and to stimulate creative thought in other persons of our community.

Let us first remove the popular misconception that creative thought is a gift which only a few selected persons in the world possess. Because the great works of art and discoveries of science, which have been made by a few individuals, attract our attention and admiration, let us not forget that the average person can also do original work. When we remember that the productive thought of the genius shows the same essential characteristics as that of the man of the street, we realize that the original work of the average person has a definite value even though it may possess less merit than that of the famous leader. More creative thinking by more people will accelerate the progress of civilization.

If we are to stimulate creative thought in more people, we must encourage them to actually try to solve difficult problems instead of accepting an easy solution or someone else's opinion. Creative thought will only appear if the problem is sufficiently difficult for the thinker, as we have pointed out before. It is all too easy to avoid the effort and unpleasantness, which accompany the attempt to solve a difficult problem, by saying to one's self, "I can't think about that," and then refusing to think about it. We all feel a strong temptation to brush aside a difficult problem and refuse to think about it. We try to forget about a problem by giving some ready-made answer, which we have heard or gained from our own experience, and let it go at that. It is very important, then, that we encourage people to be willing and eager to tackle the solution of a difficult problem. This is the first essential condition of creative thought.

When a person is ready to grapple with a hard problem, it is imperative that he be allowed sufficient time in which to solve it. The thinker should have a sense of leisure. He should be more interested in the quality of his work than in meeting a deadline. If a person has a fixed time limit, he is apt to give an incomplete answer and not try for the best solution, because his time limit has expired. The creative thinker should be allowed to feel that he can think about the problem from all angles, without being rushed. He should have the sense of leisure that he is free to consider his problem as much as he wants, without having to meet a definite time limit. This is another essential condition of creative thought.

Personal Characteristics and Attitudes Favorable for Creative Thinking

Certain general characteristics and attitudes are favorable to creative thinking. A person's interest in solving a difficult problem should be increased as much as possible. Not only should you be greatly interested in starting a problem, but your interest should be sustained through the different stages until the final revision or verification has been made and the problem is completely finished. The thinker's eagerness to reach a correct solution should never wane until that has been accomplished.

An interest in solving a problem is not enough. It should

be accompanied by the ability for sustained effort. The successful thinker must develop the capacity for prolonged, hard work. He must be willing to work overtime to follow out a new lead if necessary. The original worker does not close his desk on the stroke of the clock, but arranges his activities according to the demands of his work. When necessary, he is willing to labor at the cost of great personal inconvenience in order to develop the implications of a new idea. We should develop our ability for sustained effort, if we wish to do original work of high quality.

Too many adults, after they get out of school, lose their ability to keep on working at a hard mental problem. When they are no longer required to give the answers to school assignments in order to get a grade, they quit trying to solve problems. They become mentally lazy. If we are to stimulate more creative thinking, we must encourage more people to attempt difficult mental problems after they leave school.

Patience is a distinct asset in productive thinking. The original worker must be willing to try any number of leads to achieve the best result. You must be willing to try again and again in spite of discouragement. Most of the great thinkers of the world have overcome many failures before they achieved success. Patience is essential for original work of the highest quality.

An attitude of caution is necessary to achieve the best creative work. The good thinker proceeds carefully both in developing the main idea and in elaborating the details. When he is gathering information, he is careful to see that his notes and records are accurate. When he gets a "hunch," he carefully follows out its implications. He works cautiously in his elaboration, revision or verification to make sure that no mistake is made. Caution and accuracy both in gathering information and in revising and checking results are important for productive work.

Another attribute which is beneficial to creative thinking is a general curiosity about many different items of one's

experience. A spirit of inquiry is helpful in obtaining original ideas. The highest type of scientific thinking has its roots
in curiosity about the world in which we live. Likewise,
curiosity about his environment prompts the artist or author
to record what he sees in some lasting medium. A general
spirit of inquiry is an important factor in stimulating the
highest type of creative thinking.

A definite attempt should be made to increase everyone's
ability to observe with wide-awake attention. Everyone
should train himself to observe with a spirit of inquiry.
The child's natural curiosity should be directed into productive channels. Although the child must learn to control
his curiosity in certain areas to conform to certain social
customs and taboos, yet in other directions his curiosity
should be constantly stimulated. Let everyone learn early
that if he complies with certain social restrictions, he is free
to explore all the other areas of his experience.

A spirit of optimism is another important characteristic
for the successful thinker. If a person is to do original work,
he must feel that he can eventually solve the problem before
him. Even if we meet with repeated failure, we must still
feel that we can eventually reach the solution. Instead of becoming discouraged, we must have confidence that we can
learn from our mistakes and will come out all right in the
end. If the thinker believes that he will eventually achieve
success, he will be motivated to keep on working and revising until he produces an invention or work of art of high
quality. All of us should develop a spirit of optimism that
we will be able to solve a difficult problem if we undertake
it.

If the thinker can develop a peace of mind he has gone
a long way toward success. The production of original work
is greatly facilitated if one can avoid worry and confusion
about matters which distract from the problem. If we can
shake ourselves free from worry over other matters, we can
accomplish far more. It is of prime importance to be able to

concentrate on a problem without being distracted by our own thoughts. All the time and energy spent in worry can be counted as lost in regard to the problem at hand. If we can apply the time and energy, which we spend in worry and confusion over irrelevant things, to the present task, we can advance much further in our work. The ability to maintain peace of mind is very important for the production of original work of the highest quality.

A personality trait which is highly important in creative thinking is a sense of humor. A spirit of intellectual play gives a person access to a wide variety of ideas. He is able to consider many different possibilities in a spirit of detachment. He takes delight in trying out new and unusual combinations of ideas. Furthermore, a sense of humor enables a person to view himself more objectively, and he does not get too wrought up over his own mistakes. The thinker with a good sense of humor is truly gifted, for he is able to view both himself and his work in better perspective. If he achieves a masterpiece he does not set himself apart from the world as better than anyone else and therefore not subject to criticism, which attitude may be highly detrimental to further work. Instead, he looks at himself more objectively. In fact, those who have produced the most original work usually have a highly developed sense of humor or spirit of intellectual play, which may be lacking in persons of less merit. People who possess but little sense of humor or intellectual play should make a distinct effort to develop it, if they wish to increase the quality of their creative thinking.

The bodily condition and feeling tone of the thinker have a definite influence on his original work. Those occasions when a person feels in the best of health may or may not be the most favorable circumstances for his creative effort. Some persons do their best work when they are partly sick and below par. As one author mentioned, he did his best work when he was partly sick, but not too sick. When he was feeling well he wished to engage in more vigorous physical activities. The state of health which may be most beneficial to one thinker may be detrimental to another. Some people do their most successful thinking when they are most fit. Others, as mentioned above, can really concentrate better when they are under par. Many people like to postpone solving a difficult problem, because they don't feel well. As a matter of fact, a number of us could do as good or better work than when we are well, if we only realized it. You should honestly try to ascertain the bodily condition under which you can achieve your best results. The greater creative thinker is willing to work whenever he can accomplish the best results, sometimes even under conditions of physical discomfort, if that is necessary.

It is well known that different persons assume various physical postures as they work. Some individuals pace the floor when they are thinking about a difficult problem. Others sit quietly at their desks when they are concentrating, while others may even lie down or relax in any easy chair. If a person finds out that certain physical postures are conducive to his best work, he should not hesitate to use them. In fact, he should make an effort to ascertain what sort of physical activity accompanies his most productive efforts. Then when he tries to solve a complicated problem he should deliberately assume the physical posture or activity which is best for him.

Likewise, each of us should try to find out what mood or emotional tone accompanies our best work. This varies widely with each person. You should make a deliberate effort to cultivate the mood or feeling tone which is most conducive to your creative thinking. Or, if you find yourself at times in a certain mood favorable for productive thinking, you should drop other distracting activities and attend to it, as much as that is possible. We cannot always do so under the pressure of daily routine, but we should make the attempt when we can.

When we consider personal attributes which hinder

creative thinking, mental laziness is probably the most detrimental. As much as possible, we should try to reason out the answers ourselves instead of accepting what others say about things. We should not become lazy when we try to figure out things, and accept the easiest answer which might suffice. We should not be satisfied with the stereotyped opinions expressed by people who are not adequately informed. It is natural for a person to avoid the effort of thinking about a problem if he doesn't have to, and can find an answer provided by someone else much more easily. We should try to avoid such mental laziness, which is detrimental to creative thought.

The person who has a tendency to project his faults on others is hampered in achieving success, because he cannot criticise his own work objectively. It is hard for anyone to admit, even to himself, that his errors are due to his own lack of foresight. We all dislike to say that we made a mistake. It is much easier to blame the inefficiency of an assistant than to admit that one's own reasoning was wrong. A thinker is often hindered in his achievement by projecting his faults on another and thus failing to discern the actual cause of the mistake. We must be on guard against this tendency in ourselves if we wish to criticise and improve our productive thinking.

Another factor which hinders a person's ability to criticise his own work is the tendency to assume the good traits of another person for one's self. If a person rests content that his work possesses all the merits of that of another thinker who has succeeded, he may overlook some grave inconsistencies. It is easy to identify one's self with another's success and to attribute merit to one's own production, which it does not possess. Let us be careful that we do not yield to the tendency to assume another's success as our own, and thus fail to discern the defects in our own work.

The creative thinker should always be ready to receive and examine the new idea. He should not be afraid to accept it, if it seems better than his former concepts, even though his professional reputation is at stake. The younger person often has the advantage over the mature thinker in that he has not committed himself by his previous writings to maintain a certain viewpoint. He is free to accept any new theory or explanation which accords with the facts, because he has not previously committed himself to any certain interpretation. The mature scholar, on the other hand, may hesitate a long while before he will admit that some of his previous work will need revision. Likewise an artist or a writer, who has established his reputation in one medium, may be unwilling to attempt a more efficient manner of expressing his ideas. Success in creative thinking demands a willingness to accept the new idea, even though one's professional reputation be at stake.

The spirit of adventure is also seen in the willingness to combine ideas taken from entirely different segments of our culture. The successful thinker is not afraid to make original combinations from various fields of knowledge. He likes to put two different ideas together in order to see what will happen, and to abide by the results. For instance, he may combine methods and techniques obtained from several different sciences in one investigation. Or the writer may make use of different literary forms in one work. The creative thinker should be alert to the advantages of such unusual combinations.

Suggestions of Means to Improve Creative Thinking

From this discussion of general attitudes and characteristics, which are beneficial to creative thinking, we will now point out some specific actions and procedures which are helpful. Let each of us endeavor to apply these measures to our own productive thought.

The creative thinker should acquire as much material and information as possible about the problem under consideration. If one is well equipped with knowledge of the work which has been done in his field, he is on the road toward an important discovery or the production of a masterpiece. Many persons find it helpful to follow a regular schedule in acquisition of the necessary information. Others may collect their information in a more or less haphazard manner.

To read all which one can find of similar work on the problem is valuable. We should know about all the important contributions, which have been made in our special field. But we should also take note of other contributions, which have been considered of less value. Sometimes an obscure work contains an important lead for original thought. We should be willing to obtain knowledge from all writings, even those which are not considered very important.

A person should master the technical aspects of his problem so that his thought is not hampered by the inability to express himself. Thus the scientist should learn the various laboratory techniques which are commonly used, so that he will not be hindered by elementary procedures. The artist should learn the different ways of using a brush and how to mix colors. The poet should practice the various verse forms, so that he can express himself easily in any medium. Often the inexperienced person is unable to give expression to his idea, because he is hampered by the inability to make use of the proper artistic, musical and literary forms. If we wish to do original work, we should be willing to spend many hours, months, or years to master the methods and techniques of our subject, so that we can freely use them.

Reading and study are not the only ways to acquire knowledge about one's special area of interest. Talking with people who have done similar work is often enlightening. From such informal conversation with persons engaged in similar work you can often gain ideas, which would probably never find their way into print. This is one big advantage of conventions, where many people, who are doing the same thing, can meet and informally exchange ideas. Attendance at scientific associations and artistic, musical, and literary societies provides this opportunity for interchange of information. The productive thinker is eager to acquire knowledge, whether he does that by reading, organized study, or conversation with others, or by a combination of all three methods.

Although we should spend much time and effort acquiring knowledge in our own field, yet we should be alert to gain information in other areas of our culture. It is a distinct advantage to know the values, techniques and viewpoints of other disciplines. If we are familiar with other methods and points of view, we are in a position to look at our problem from a new angle. We should make an effort to learn about other areas of present-day culture. For instance, a person doing research in psychology might find training in physics to be helpful, especially in the field of vision. Or a knowledge of sculpture might help in painting. By combining the methods of different disciplines one is in a favored position to obtain an original idea, or approach.

Likewise the thinker should learn about work which has been done on his particular problem by other investigators employing different or opposite methods, viewpoints, and objectives. The thinker can thus observe the various approaches, and so will be able to decide on a proper course of procedure from a different angle. When a new approach is made, sometimes a complicated problem becomes clear, which otherwise would appear insoluble. It is important to read widely about different attempts which have been made to solve the problem under consideration.

Another way of getting a new slant on one's problem is to talk to people who have never done any work in the field and who thus have a fresh, naïve point of view. In trying to explain to the untutored listener, you are often made aware of certain obscurities and incongruities in your work which you have overlooked before. As you try to describe your work in non-technical language, you may become aware of logical inconsistencies, which you had previously over-looked. Also, the questions which the non-professional person asks are often helpful and present a refreshing viewpoint to the thinker. Such questions may make him suddenly aware of re-examining his fundamental premises. It is well for every scholar to stop and think over some of the fundamental assumptions, which he takes for granted.

Artistic production is frequently initiated by sensory stimulation. There is a large variation among individuals in this respect. If an artist or a writer knows that certain types of scenery prompt him to do good work, he should take a notebook and jot down ideas, when he knows that he is going to such a place. Or if he is going to a concert where he will hear certain types of music which are helpful, he should be ready to record any ideas. If you know that certain types of situations are conducive to your best work, you should let nothing interfere with the recording of any new thoughts which you might happen to have.

Certain affective states are also conducive to creative thinking. The artist or scientist should do what he can to get himself in the proper mood to work. Sometimes a person can deliberately induce a favorable mood. For instance, some persons find the physical activity of sitting down at the desk, clearing off irrelevant objects, and getting out the necessary material and apparatus to be helpful. Or a sculptor may find that putting on his frock and getting out his instruments and clay suggest the proper mood for working. If an inventor goes into his study and takes out his models and his tools, he may find that he begins to think more easily about his invention. The routine of preparing for work or other routines may be effective in producing the proper mood or emotional tone. The thinker should deliberately perform such acts which create the atmosphere for his clearest thinking.

The work of the novelist, poet, musician or painter is greatly influenced by the knowledge obtained from the social and cultural environment around him. Every thinker should stop and realize the environmental factors which are influencing him. If he is aware of certain conditions which may color the nature of his thought, he is in a position to critically evaluate the environmental forces about him, and to bring out new and original interpretations in his work. The thinker should also realize that too strict adherence to artistic, scientific, or social conventions may hinder his creative thought. While accurate work requires a realization of these demands, a person should not follow them too closely if he wishes to do work, which is highly original. On the other hand, if we disregard such conventions too much, our achievements become eccentric and may even be rejected by society. The really great creative thinker is one who is able to achieve the delicate balance between adherence to many of the conventions of his art or science, and the disregard of others. Some great thinkers, because of their disregard of the contemporary conventions, do work which is not appreciated during their lifetime. Their work is more in keeping with that of a later generation, and they become well-known after their death. The creative worker should carefully consider his production in the light of the standards of the discipline which he follows, but he should be willing to make the exception where that seems to be beneficial.

If you wish to do original work, you should allow a certain amount of time in your daily routine for solitude and meditation. It is often valuable to indulge in a certain amount of reverie and autistic thinking. The mind can thus be at ease and often the unusual and worthwhile idea comes to one's attention.

How many of us nowadays ever sit down in a chair to devote an hour or two to nothing but reverie and meditation? In our Western culture such idleness is severely frowned upon. We feel that we should constantly be accomplishing something concrete and specific, either at our job or at some chosen recreational activity. If we do sit down in a chair by ourselves in a room, it is usually to read a newspaper or magazine, or else take a nap. Very seldom are we content to sit in a chair and do nothing but let our thoughts come freely as they will, without any definite plan. In fact, so severely does our Western civilization frown upon any such activity that we usually condemn a person who does it to any large extent and term him as abnormal, as either feeble-minded or else as psychopathic. If we have a friend who spends an hour or two a day in such idleness, we immediately become concerned about his health and think he should be sent to a psychiatrist.

Did you ever notice how many people rush to buy a newspaper or a magazine before they board a train, even though they may be commuters, with only a short trip of half an hour or an hour? They are afraid to sit alone with their own thoughts for a few minutes. They are so strongly convinced that such idleness, for only a short period, is to be sternly condemned. Some of these commuters may feel that the train ride is their only chance to read the newspaper in a busy day. Do they ever stop to consider that a half hour with their own thoughts might be far more valuable to them than reading the newspaper? Although they derive pleasure from the sensational news of the average paper or magazine, do they ever stop to realize they might also derive pleasure from their own reveries? At various times in the history of civilization people have realized the importance of living with one's own thoughts for certain periods of time. Some of the oriental religions have emphasized that. Because the tempo of our western life has largely crowded out such periods of reverie and meditation, that does not mean they are unimportant. Some persons are very unhappy when they board a train or bus and have to be inactive with nothing to read. Instead of chafing at their bad luck, let them welcome such moments as important opportunities in their lives. Let them know that a train ride in which they do the thinking is far more important than passively reading a newspaper or magazine.

In solving a complicated problem we should plan to stop and rest from time to time, which is just as important as having certain hours for concentration. Often we become tense when we work hard at a problem and can't solve it. If we stop for a while, we can look at the whole matter with a new slant. These periods when we discontinue working can take the form of complete rest, as lying down, or some form of light physical exercise. Both scientists and inventors, as well as artists and writers, assert that they frequently obtain some of their best ideas when they are leisurely walking. Other types of recreation may be beneficial. Some types of passive entertainment, as reading a novel or listening to a concert, are helpful to some people. On the other hand, such recreation, as dancing, playing cards or other games, and those amusements, which involve constant interaction with other people, according to fixed rules, would not favor the occurrence of original ideas. If a person is actively talking or responding to others, he would not have time to make a note of a new idea, even if it occurred to him. He would probably forget about it rather than inconvenience himself and others by recording it. If the creative thinker wishes to plan his recreation to favor his production of original work, he will engage in those activities which he can passively enjoy by himself or which include light physical activity. He will also find certain types of routine physical work beneficial. He will avoid the kinds of amusements which demand constant social interaction with other persons, according to fixed rules, as dancing and games. However, such type of social interaction found in informal general discussions, may be beneficial.

A good time for obtaining new ideas is when we first awaken in the morning. That is a particularly favorable time for perceiving new approaches to a problem. Many persons have stated how they got the hunch, for which they were searching, at that hour. Such new ideas frequently come while the person is engaged in the routine preparations for the day. While many people are often hurried at that hour, they should always take the time to jot down any sudden ideas, which they happen to have. Often a very short notation is sufficient to recall it to a person's mind, whereas if he didn't write down anything at all, he would probably completely forget it. Also periods of half-sleep, as when an individual partially awakens during the night, or dozes off for a nap in the daytime, are occasions when one should watch for new ideas. If a person will jot down what he happens to think at such times, he will be amply repaid for the small amount of time and effort involved.

In fact, the creative thinker who does the best work, is always alert to remember a new idea whenever it might occur to him, no matter what he is doing. If he closes his desk for a while and takes part in some form of light physical exercise, he should be alert to remember any novel approach which might occur to him while he is so engaged. If he is reading a novel or listening to a concert, he should be ready to recall any hunch which might flash upon him, and should make a definite notation of it. Even if he is doing some sort of routine physical work, he should never hesitate to take time off to jot down some memorandum of an idea which he might get. Some people even find it helpful to do other kinds of mental work, when they stop working on the problem which they are trying to solve.

"Form the notebook habit." That is one of the most important pieces of advice for the creative thinker. We are often tempted to let a good idea slip away from us, because we don't want to make the effort to memorize it or record it on paper. We should overcome such inertia, and form the habit of always being ready to stop and memorize, or record in one way or another, any good idea which happens to occur, even though it may seem a little far-fetched at the time. We may not be able to tell the real significance of an idea on the spur of the moment, without much critical evaluation, but if it might possibly be worthwhile, we should keep it. If we record an idea, we always have the opportunity to criticize it later and see if it should be rejected.

No one doubts the value of forming favorable living habits to do a large amount of successful work. The development of favorable routines for worthwhile achievements is highly important, as the lives of the leaders in various fields exemplify. One's manner of living and of organizing his work and his time forms the groundwork for his future success, if it is favorable, and for his failure, if it is poor. Yet in spite of the tremendous importance of habits in success, if they are too fixed, they may interfere with a person's creative thinking. Sometimes a variation in one's routine and personal habits may promote new ideas. Although most people object to changing their daily schedule, yet such a variation is often highly important for creative work. If you do not seem to make much progress with your complicated problems, you might arbitrarily make some changes in your manner of life. This may involve some expenditure of effort and money, yet the results can well be worth the cost. For instance, sometimes a trip, in which you temporarily assume a different mode of life, is helpful. Or if you remain at home, you can make alterations in your work or recreations. Even if the new habits have no direct bearing on the problem, yet the factor of change in your personal life may be sufficient to stimulate original ideas.

We should be careful that we do not permit our mental set or way of looking at things to interfere with our creative thinking. Sometimes our established beliefs can prove detrimental in creative work. It is frequently an unpleasant process to stop and consider whether some of the things which we have always believed are really true. Yet if we are willing to make the effort, we will find that we can often approach a difficult problem from a new angle. Sometimes we get in the habit of thinking along certain lines, because we have studied much of the work of certain scientists, artists, or inventors. We may find ourselves unduly influenced by the work of a certain individual in our field of research, or art, or literature. In such cases, we should make a deliberate attempt to acquaint ourselves more widely with the works of other leaders in our area of endeavor. This may involve considerable time and effort and we may feel that we are wasting our energies, because it is not directly connected with the problem at hand. Yet such an attempt to gain a new viewpoint often leads to a new approach to the problem, and our expenditure of effort is more than justified.

Often the original thinker falls short of his best work, because he is too lazy to think out the full implications of his idea. As a result his work may bear obvious defects, which he could have easily eliminated if he had been willing to make the effort to revise or verify it. Or he may fail to reach an important discovery, which he could have made if he had been willing to follow out the full implications of his idea. It takes effort, which is often unpleasant, to carry out the full significance of a new solution. The thinker should be willing to proceed through the tedious task of submitting his idea and comparing it with the standards of science, art, literature, or music, as the case may be. In order to produce original work of the highest quality, you must be willing to endure the unpleasantness of fatigue, which accompanies a thorough revision or verification of an idea, even though the process requires days, months, or even years to complete.

It is not enough to have a notebook accessible during one's waking hours, but on retiring the thinker should place it near his bed. One of the most favorable periods in the twenty-four hours is immediately after awakening in the morning, before one has become involved in the daily duties. Likewise, moments of half-sleep, as when one has just retired for the night, or when he awakens during the night, are also advantageous. If a person can rouse himself at such times to make some sort of a notation of a pertinent idea, he may be amply rewarded by finding the next morning that he has obtained a new approach or solution to the problem. The potential gains from the notebook habit far overshadow the small inconvenience and little time which it consumes.

We should also form the habit of asking ourselves questions about the things which interest us. You should ask yourself as many different questions as possible, and then try to answer each one of them by yourself. If you cannot do that, then consult the works and references of other people. One should never hesitate to ask questions about ordinary things, which most people take for granted. That is the way some great discoveries are made, as when Newton asked, "Why does an apple fall toward the ground?" Thousands of people had seen apples fall toward the ground, without bothering to ask "Why?" Or if they did ask the question, they did not bother to answer it. This shows the importance not only of asking a question, but also of searching until the correct answer is found. Everyone who wishes to do original work should form the habit of asking questions about ordinary things, as well as about unusual events, and then trying to answer his inquiries by himself.

Procedures for the Classroom

Let us now pass to some of the more specific procedures, which can be instituted in the classroom to improve the creative thinking of the next generation. At the outset let it be said that every educator from the kindergarten to the graduate school should always be on the alert to notice any new ideas proposed by young people, and to encourage that individual to the utmost of his ability. Every educator should consider that fostering original work in the youth of the world is his most important duty, even more important than teaching information. The future of our whole civilization depends on the quality of the creative thinking done by the next generation.

With that in mind let us train teachers to have an adventurous spirit in their teaching so as to impart that spirit to the pupils. If we have teachers who are eager to explore the mysteries of the world about them, they will fill their students with the same desire to discover the new, and to explain the unknown. It is evident that children imitate their elders, and if they are thrown in daily contact with persons who are interested themselves in finding out the cause of things and in doing original work, they will be stimulated to do likewise.

Even if a teacher doesn't possess a general curiosity, he should simulate it in the classroom. He should pretend that he is interested in such things as how a goldfish swims, and how water boils. If he pretends that he is interested in producing an original drawing or painting, or in writing an original story or poem, the children will imitate him and do likewise. The duty of the teacher to incite a spirit of inquiry is not confined to the elementary grades, but extends all through the high school and college levels. If the instructor shows by his actions that he is eager to inquire about the objects of his environment, that personal example will do more to encourage his students or pupils to do likewise than any amount of talking would do. Let the teachers' colleges and educational institutions revise their curriculums to impress on the future teachers the overwhelming importance of showing in their own lives and by their own examples that spirit of inquiry, which they wish to engender in their pupils. If they do not actually feel it, let them at least simulate curiosity while they are in the classroom.

We are all capable of creative thinking of more or less merit, although we are not all able to reach the highest levels. So implanted is the prevalent idea that most of us cannot do original work that we should make a definite effort to reduce the fears of both teachers and pupils that their own creative ideas are absent or negligible. Let everyone realize that each of us can do some sort of original work, which has more or less merit. That is another responsibility of teachers' colleges and courses in education: to remove the erroneous belief that the creative work of teachers and their pupils is negligible or not worthwhile. The aim of courses of education should be to remove that fear and to substitute for it a full realization that everyone can do some kind of original work. The ordinary person's sense of futility about doing something original should give way to a feeling of confidence.

Beginning with the elementary grades, one way to instill that confidence is to encourage the children to articulate about their whimsies and fancies. Urge them to write down the things which they imagine in the form of simple stories or poems. Or let them take a pencil or paintbrush and depict what they think. Or give them a crude musical instrument and let them try to compose a piece. If they feel the urge, encourage them to dramatize their ideas or make up a dance. If a child has something concrete to show for what he thought, he gains confidence and is more apt to try again. If a child gives overt expression to his imaginative ideas, the teacher can show appreciation and thus give him the necessary encouragement. From the early years the child should be urged to express his whimsies and fancies in some form or other.

In every classroom, from the kindergarten through the graduate school, formal training should always be accompanied by the opportunity for creative efforts. The importance of this fact should not be overlooked in planning any curriculum from the grades to the lectures or laboratory schedules of the university. In many educational programs the opportunities for original productions are sadly neglected. For instance, while training in the rules and syllogisms of traditional logic leads to accurate thinking, it does not lead to productive work. Something more than that is required. The student should be urged to go further and do creative work. Not only logic, but other formal disciplines may crowd out the opportunities for original productions. In planning any curriculum, we should be careful to see that does not happen.

An instructor should lead his students to approach a problem by viewing it as a whole from as many different angles as possible. The proper orientation is often the keynote to success in any line of work. If we realize from the beginning that several different approaches are possible, then if one angle is unsuccessful, we won't spend too much time on it. We will try something else for a while, even if we return to the first approach later on. The proper orientation to the problem is highly important for achievement in any endeavor, whether in science or art.

The use of proper thought models is valuable to prepare students for producing original work. If an instructor presents the students with a careful selection of the methods which can be employed, he can steer them away from futile attempts. Whether he is presenting music, art, or literature, or any of the sciences, the instructor should be aware that he has a large responsibility to present the best thought models. It is not enough for the student to know the results, but even more, how the results were obtained. The would-be inventor should not only understand the principle of how an appliance operates, but even more he should be shown the technique by which it was made. Methods, then, are more important than results to give the student the necessary background for creative work.

The typical "appreciation" course aims to cover a lot of material and present only a superficial survey of a number of masterpieces. For many a student, this is the only contact he ever has with a certain type of music, art, or literature. For this reason, while a certain amount of time can be spent in general survey, the instructor should select several masterpieces and devote the time to go into great detail as to the methods and techniques by which they were produced. Thus, the student can gain some comprehension of what he would actually have to do, if he were to produce a masterpiece himself.

Frequently our "appreciation" courses, in pointing out the cultural influence and excellence of the masterpiece, give the average student the opinion that such wonders can only result from "inspiration," which is bestowed upon the genius. He is led to believe that such work can only be achieved by a very few people who are so "inspired." As a consequence it is futile for him to even try to do any original work of that type. If, on the other hand, the elementary "appreciation" course points out the laborious methods and techniques by which the masterpiece was produced, the average student will see that such actions are not so completely different from the things he himself does, and his sense of reverence and awe will be reduced. He will gain self-confidence and will be encouraged to try some original work of his own.

Not only their pupils but teachers and instructors themselves often have the belief that the masterpiece can only be the result of "inspiration" to a "genius." Moreover, the well-known musicians, artists, and literary writers are partly responsible for this belief that their work is set far apart from what the average man could possibly do. When asked how they produce their work, many of them relapse into some vague explanation of "inspiration" or "revelation," either from some supernatural power or from the subconscious. It is very gratifying to feel that one has accomplished something no one else could do, so they naturally talk about their work in a manner to increase that sense of reverence and awe which the world is already willing to attribute to their achievements. As a result, they are frequently allowed exceptions from the rules which apply to the ordinary person, because of artistic or poetic "temperament."

Much can be done to dispel this sense of awe, if the time is taken to analyze a masterpiece and show in detail the methods which the artist or author used. For instance, in tracing the development of a famous painting the instructor should show how the artist obtained the main idea, perhaps from something in his personal environment. Some idea of how the preliminary sketches were made should be indicated, as well as how the particular type of paint was selected and mixed. Both the type of canvas and the different kinds of brushes, with the various strokes employed, should be noted. The way in which the artist began his picture, whether he painted the background or the foreground first, or began in one corner or the other could be studied, as well as his manner of revising it. While there are very few masterpieces concerning which such information is available, yet the instructor would only need one or two such examples in his elementary appreciation course. The important thing is to trace in detail how at least one famous artist or author or composer worked. If a student is shown how a masterpiece is "manufactured" step by step, he will cease to think of it as something beyond his reach, and will gain confidence that he, too, could do some original work. Although a general survey of the art or literature or music of a period provides some very worthwhile information, yet if the elementary appreciation course stimulates even a small proportion of the students to do original work, it will have been far more valuable.

Some courses are now given to teach the various techniques employed in writing literature, composing music, or doing art work. Too often these courses deal with only certain technical phases in the production of a masterpiece, and they fail to show the development of the process from the very beginning of the original idea. In the study of poetry techniques, for instance, a knowledge of verse forms and types of metre covers only a small phase of the total process of writing a poem. Such information can only be gained by studying in detail how a famous poem was created from the time the author started to search for an idea. More books tracing the development of more masterpieces should be made available as required reading for all literary, art, and music courses.

Let the educators, then, impress upon young people the fundamental similarity which exists between the creative thinking of the average person and that of the famous man of letters. The chief defect of much of our educational system to-day is that more emphasis is placed on the establishment of behavior norms than on the production of original work. In fact, many teachers confess that their chief aim is to have the pupils return the information which they give. Teachers may even be annoyed when a pupil presents an original answer which differs from what is expected, because it does not fit in with the rest of their scoring scheme for grades. They have to stop and think themselves how the unusual answer should be treated. The assertion is often made that the classes are too large for teachers to handle, and hence they cannot take the time to adequately deal with the original answer. They are thus forced to try to regiment the pupils to give the same type of answers on their tests in a routine manner, which is easy to grade.

Let every teacher, instructor, and professor stop and ask himself the question, "How do I teach?" "What are the methods which I employ?" Let each one face the question, whether he insists that his pupils or students slavishly repeat his talks or lectures or the textbook assignments. Let him ask, "Do I give the highest grade to the student or pupil who can repeat things I taught him almost word for word on tests and examinations?" "Or do I give the highest grades to the one who is less accurate from the standpoint of remembering everything I said, but who expresses some new idea of his own, even though I do not exactly agree with it?" If each teacher answers these questions honestly, the majority will give an affirmative answer to the first one. Many may deceive themselves that they favor the original answer, but they allow so little opportunity for creative thinking in the classroom that it seldom occurs, and when they observe an original answer they do not give due credit.

Both teachers in the early grades and professors in colleges should be careful not to let their own biases and prejudices affect the information which they give to the students. It is easy for an instructor to fall into the habit of presenting material from his own point of view, unless he is careful not to do so. A teacher should always make a definite effort to present other arguments and viewpoints regarding the same data. The conflict which arises in the student's mind, when he is presented with different descriptions or explanations of the same data, is one of the best incentives for encouraging him to do original thinking. On the other hand, if he is only presented with one viewpoint, such as that which the instructor favors, he will passively accept that without trying to think for himself.

Not only the teacher, but also the student, should be on guard lest his personal bias and prejudice affect his work. Frequently, a student refuses to give adequate consideration to information he obtains in college, if that conflicts with his pet ideas and prejudices. He is disdainful of theories which don't accord with his already established beliefs. Every student should realize that even if he does not agree with what he hears in the classroom, at least it is a broadening experience to examine the arguments behind the other interpretations. Every student should be duly impressed with the importance of being open-minded about all information he receives in the classroom, as for instance economic, religious, and political theories. He should realize the importance of thoroughly understanding different theories, even though he does not agree with the conclusions. The student who is willing to study all points of view enough to understand them is the one who is best qualified to do original thinking.

In presenting information to be learned or memorized

in the classroom care should be taken to point out the difference between those facts which have been proved and those hypotheses and theories which have not been definitely established. Some assertions, which have not been definitely established, are made so commonly that we come to assume they are facts even when they have not been proved. Such confusion can lead to grave errors and misconceptions. This failure to differentiate between the actual fact and the assumed theory may be a big obstacle in achieving a high quality of productive thought. If a person believes that a certain assertion is already established, he will lack the motivation to re-examine the premises and do original thinking about it. On the other hand, if the student is made to realize that a certain assumption is not yet proved, that may be the incentive which will eventually lead him to make an original discovery or invention.

Teachers should show pupils, beginning in the early grades, how to define a problem and keep testing each suggestion systematically. For instance, in a practical problem the teacher could point out the different ways it might be solved and encourage the pupil to try out the various possibilities. After he has tried the different suggestions, the teacher could let the child decide for himself which was the best. If such habits of thought are established in early childhood, they will be a distinct advantage for later life.

Beginning with the lower grades, certain periods should be set aside for passive contemplation and daydreaming in planning the school curriculum. Some of the tasks which now crowd the school program should be omitted in order that each pupil might have the opportunity from time to time to think about anything which interests him. Each period of "daydreaming" should be followed by the instruction that the pupils reproduce or give a record of their thoughts in some manner, as by art work, writing, dancing, playing a musical instrument, and such. The important thing is to make the child get in the habit of recording what he thinks.

This has the advantage that it makes the pupil appreciate the value of his imagination, and at the same time it discourages excessive idle daydreaming, which produces no result. If the child can see his own ideas expressed in concrete form, he will be encouraged to keep on trying.

How Parents May Help

Outside of the classroom parents can do much to foster creative thinking in the child. Most of the suggestions for stimulating creative thought in school apply equally well to the child's home environment. The parent should always be ready to give the youngster proper encouragement to do original work. You should not be too busy to take the time to show proper appreciation for his original work. If the child's first efforts to create something new are spurned, he may be discouraged from trying further. Every father and mother should always be alert to notice the child's creative work and give him the proper assistance.

Whenever a child shows initiative along one line, it is up to the parent to furnish the necessary materials. It does not matter if the materials are cheap, for the important thing is to permit the youngster to express himself in the medium he prefers. For instance, drawing and finger painting are common methods which frequently appear, and the necessary paints, crayons, or pencils can easily be provided. The clay to enable the child to model his original ideas is easily obtained. Older children may like to write poems, stories, or even make up their own plays. Several playmates can be encouraged to do such things together, and give each other incentive for working out original ideas. Thus, several children could get together and write poems and stories and read them to each other. Or they could paint or draw together and show each other the pictures produced.

You should try to avoid telling your child what to paint or draw or construct. When he asks, "What shall I make?" you should always tell him to try some of his own ideas first.

It may take more effort on your part to give the necessary suggestions to prompt the child to work out his own ideas, but the results are far more worthwhile. It is often a big temptation, when a youngster asks, "What shall I do or make?" to name some common object for him to copy, so he will be quiet for a while. Instead of answering that question for the youngster, you should always be ready to spend the effort necessary to make the child answer it himself.

Likewise, when the child asks a question to obtain information, the parent should try to make the child answer it himself, if that is practical. The experience of reasoning out the information is frequently far more valuable than the information itself. As mentioned before, such procedure is most effective to encourage creative thinking, but it consumes more time and effort on the part of the parent. If the question is beyond the child's capacity or if he is unable to answer it after trying, then you should give as correct an answer as you can. Children's questions should never go unanswered, if possible. Much harm can be done if their queries are ignored, for that stifles curiosity. As we mentioned before, productive thinking depends to a large extent on a generalized curiosity about one's environment. You will do your child a great service if you see that his questions are always answered either by himself or by an adult.

After all, if the great thinkers of the world did not have confidence that their own thoughts were more valuable than things they copied, they would not have spent most of their lives working out the great contributions to civilization. This feeling of confidence in one's own original ideas should have its beginning in childhood, and the parents can do as much to encourage that attitude as the teacher in the classroom.

You can do much to foster creative thinking in the next generation, if you allow your child to indulge in a certain amount of reverie without interruptions, just as you permit other recreations. The potential value of the youngster's daydreams should be considered as important as playing with blocks, dolls or toy trains. If you always require your child to make some record of his phantasies, either by writing his ideas or by drawing, modelling, or some other means, such periods of meditation will be most beneficial. By early forming the habit of recording his reveries, no matter how fantastic, the child will be steered away from excessive indulgence in the futile type of daydreaming, which leads to nowhere. On the other hand, the formation of the habit of making some sort of a record of one's imaginative thoughts or reveries is a valuable asset for the person who wishes to do successful original work, since the productive thinker's best "hunches" often come during such periods. Let every parent, then, allow his child certain periods for phantasy and reverie, which should always be followed by having the child record his imaginative ideas in some way. Since the average child spends much more time at home than at school, the parent has more opportunity than the teacher for encouraging creative thinking. More efficient creative thought in the next generation will do much to advance our culture.

Summary

A program to improve creative thinking in ourselves and others should include: first, to stimulate and encourage people to tackle complicated and difficult problems; and second, to develop a sense of leisure and a certain amount of freedom from daily routine for solving such complicated problems. It is important for us to realize that we all are capable of creative thinking of more or less merit.

Certain general characteristics and attitudes are advantageous for original work, as the development of strong interest in the area of investigation, and the desire to reach a correct solution. One must be willing to work hard and not count the hours. Patience, optimism, and caution in examining all the facts are helpful. One should develop a sense of humor and a spirit of intellectual play. Each individual should find out what states of health or mood are most favorable for his own work and try to do his thinking at such times. The thinker should be ready to accept new ideas even if they conflict with his established professional standing, or tradition. Too strict adherence to artistic, scientific, or social conventions hinder the creative activity of the mind.

The original thinker will find certain specific activities beneficial in his work. By reading and observation he should collect information about the problem, as well as by talking to other people who have done similar work. Information in other fields of interest is also valuable. Likewise, answering the naïve questions of persons who have never worked within the area of investigation is often helpful to gain a new viewpoint. We should allow a certain amount of time for meditation and autistic thinking in our daily schedule. We should spend some of our leisure time in meditation or autistic thinking in an easy chair instead of spending it all in activities of the conventional forms of recreation. Even when we are engaged in other kinds of mental work, we should be on the watch for new ideas in regard to our problem, if they should occur to us. Variation in one's daily routine and personal habits, may produce the opportunity for valuable "hunches." We should form the habit of asking ourselves questions about the things in the environment which interest us, and even more important, answering our own questions. We should never hesitate to ask questions about the ordinary things which most people take for granted. At all times we should keep a notebook handy to jot down an idea, not only during the daytime, but also by one's bed at night for any "hunches" which might come during the night, and especially on awakening in the morning. Let us never be too busy to jot down what appears to be a good idea, or, if we can't do that, to spend a few minutes memorizing it so that we can recall it later.

Procedures in the classroom can do much to promote creative thought in the next generation. Educators should be alert for new ideas proposed by young people. Schools of education should train teachers to have a spirit of inquiry to inspire youth. Every effort should be made to reduce the fears of teachers and pupils that their creative efforts are absent or negligible, and confidence in their own ability to do original work should be developed. They should be urged to record their fancies and reveries in some manner or medium. Very often formal education is too much absorption and learning, and not enough production, expression and opportunity for creative work. Students should be taught to view a problem from as many different angles as possible. Elementary "appreciation" courses in art or literature should not only present a general survey of the subject, but should also include a few objective examples of how a masterpiece has been produced to show similarity between the students' own creative thinking and that of the famous author or artist. Let the student realize that great creative thinking is not such a "mysterious" process as some believe. Teachers should be alert not to allow their own biases and prejudices affect the knowledge, which they present in the classroom. Likewise, students should be alert not to let their own biases and prejudices affect their willingness to understand other viewpoints. A certain amount of time should be provided in the school schedule for daydreaming and autistic thinking, and then the pupils should be asked to record their reveries and fancies in any way they wish, as art work, writing, music, dramatic work, and such.

Parents should encourage the child in creative work at home. They should refrain from telling him what to do in order to make him express his own creative ideas. They should allow the child a certain amount of time for daydreaming which should usually be followed by asking him to record his reveries in whatever manner or medium he prefers. The youngster's original work should be encouraged more than what he merely copies. Parents should stimulate children to really try to answer their own questions; then, if they can't, to ask adults, but not to forget about them.

The future progress of civilization depends on the quality of the creative thinking in the world during the years to come.

BIBLIOGRAPHY

1. ACH, N. *Uber die Willenstatigheit und das Denken.* Gottingen, 1905.
2. ADAMS, C. W. The age at which scientists do their best work. Isis, 1945–46, 36, 166–69.
3. ALEXANDER, S. The creative process in the artist's mind. Brit. J. Psych. 1926, 17, 305–21.
4. ALLPORT, G. W. Effect: a secondary principle of learning. Psych. Rev. 1946, 53, 335–47.
5. ALPERT, A. The solving of problem-situations by pre-school children. Teach. Coll. Contrib. Educ. C. U. 1928, No. 323.
6. BAHLE, J. Einfall und Inspiration im musikalischen Schaffen. Arch. ges. Psych. 1934, 90, 495–503.
7. BAHLE, J. Zur Psychologie des Einfalls und der Inspiration im musikalischen Schaffen. Acta Psych. Hague, 1935, 1, 7–29.
8. BARTLETT, F. C. Program for experiments on thinking. Quart. J. Psych. 1950, 2, 145–52.
9. BENHAM, E. The creative activity. Brit. J. Psych. 1929, 20, 59–65.
10. BENTLEY, M. Where does thinking come in? Am. J. Psych. 1943, 56, 354–80.
11. BILLINGS, M. L. Problem-solving in different fields of endeavor. Am. J. Psych., 1934, 46, 259–72.
12. BINET, A. *Psychology of Reasoning.* Chicago: Open Court, 1899.
13. BIRCH, H. G. and RABINOWITZ, H. S. The negative effect of previous experience on productive thinking. J. Exp. Psych. 1951, 41, 121–5.
14. BJORKSTEN, J. The limitation of creative years. Sci. Mon. 1946, 62, 94.
15. BLANSHARD, B. *The Nature of Thought.* N.Y.: Macmillan, 1940.
16. BLOOM, B. S. and BRODER, L. J. Problem-solving processes of college students. Chicago: Univ. Chicago Suppl. Educ. Mon., 1950, No. 73.

17. BORAAS, J. *Teaching to Think*. N.Y.: Macmillan, 1929.
18. BRITT, S. H. *Social Psychology of Modern Life*. N.Y.: Rinehart, 1941.
19. BURT, C. The development of reasoning in school children. J. Exp. Ped. 1919, 5, 68–77, 121–7.
20. BURTT, E. A. *Principles and Problems of Right Thinking*. N.Y.: Harper, 1931.
21. CANE, F. Fostering creative work. Prog. Educ. 1931, 8, 199–202.
22. CARPENTER, W. B. *Mental Physiology*. London: King, 1874.
23. CARR, H. A. Psychology, *A Study of Mental Activity*. N.Y.: Longmans, Green, 1925.
24. CHANT, S. N. An objective experiment in reasoning. Am. J. Psych. 1933, 45, 282–91.
25. CHRISTOF, C. Formulation and elaboration of thought-problems. Am. J. Psych. 1939, 52, 161–85.
26. CLAPAREDE, E. La genese de l'hypothese: etude experimental. Arch. de Psych. 1934, 24, 1–155.
27. COMMINS, W. D. *Principles of Educational Psychology*. N.Y.: Ronald, 1937.
28. COWELL, H. Process of musical creation. Am. J. Psych. 1926, 37, 233–6.
29. DASHIELL, J. F. A physiological-behavioristic description of thinking. Psych. Rev. 1925, 32, 54–73.
30. DELACROIX, H. *Psychologie de l'Art*. Paris: Libraire Felix Alcan, 1927.
31. DEWEY, J. *How We Think*. N.Y.: Heath, 1910.
32. DIMNET, E. *Art of Thinking*. N.Y.: Simon & Schuster, 1929.
33. DOIG, D. Creative music; music composed to illustrate musical problems. J. Educ. Rev. 1942, 36, 241–53.
34. DOWNEY, J. E. *Creative Imagination*. N.Y.: Harcourt, Brace, 1929.
35. DUNCKER, K. On problem-solving. Trans. by Lynne I. Lees, Psych. Mon. 1945, 58, No. 270.
36. DUNCKER, K. and KRECHEVSKY, I. On solution achievement. Psych. Rev. 1939, 46, 176–185.
37. DUNCKER, K. A qualitative (experimental and theoretical) study of productive thinking (solving of comprehensible problems). Ped. Sem. 1926, 33, 642–708.
38. DUNN, M. F. *Psychology of Reasoning*. Baltimore: Wilkins, 1926.
39. DURKIN, H. E. Trial and error, gradual analysis, and sudden reorganization. Arch. Psych. 1937, No. 210.

40. EINDHOVEN, J. and VINAKE, W. E. Creative process in painting. J. Gen. Psych. 1952, 47, 139–164.

41. ELSENHAUS, T. Theorie der phantasie. Arch. f. d. ges. Psych. 1911, 22, 30–39.

42. FARNSWORTH, P. Musical eminence and year of birth. J. Aesthet. 1945, 4, 107–9.

43. FEHR, H. *Enquete de l'Enseignement Mathematique.* Paris: Gauther-Villars 1912.

44. FEIBLEMAN, J. K. The psychology of the artist. J. Psych. 1945, 19, 165–89.

45. FISHER, S. C. The process of generalizing abstraction; and its product, the general concept. Psych. Mon. 1916, 21, No. 90.

46. FLESCH, R. *The Art of Clear Thinking.* N.Y.: Harper, 1951.

47. GALLI, E. La conscienza nella formazione dell'opera d'arte. Riv. di. psicol. 1932, 27, 107–14, 185–193, 275–84.

48. GESELL, A. *Genius, Giftedness, and Growth. The March of Medicine.* N.Y. Acad. of Med. Lectures to the Laity. N.Y.: Columbia Univ. Press, 1943.

49. GHISELIN, B. *The Creative Process.* Berkeley, Los Angeles: Univ. Calif. Press 1952.

50. GIBSON, E. J. and McGARVEY, H. R. Experimental studies of thought and reasoning. Psy. Bull. 1937, 34, 327–50.

51. GILBERT, E. J. *Travail Intellectuel (et) Invention.* Paris: Biologica, 1945.

52. GLASER, E. M. An experiment in the development of critical thinking. N.Y. Columbia Teach. Coll. Contrib. Educ. 1941, No. 843.

53. GORDON, K. Imagination: a psychological study. Introduction. J. Gen. Psych. 1935, 12, 194–207.

54. GRIFFITHS, R. *A Study of Imagination in Early Childhood.* London: Kegan Paul, 1935.

55. GRIPPEN, V. B. A study of creative artistic imagination in children by the constant contact procedure. Psych. Mon. 1933, 45, No. 200.

56. GUETZKOW, H. An analysis of the operation of set in problem-solving behavior. J. Gen. Psych. 1951, 45, 219–44.

57. GUILFORD, J. P. Creativity. Amer. Psych. 1950, 5, 444–54.

58. HADAMARD, J. *The Psychology of Invention in the Mathematical Field.* Princeton: Princeton Univ. Press, 1945.

59. HARDING, R. E. M. *An Anatomy of Inspiration; with an Appendix on the Birth of a Poem.* Cambridge: Heffer, 1942.

60. HARGREAVES, H. L. The "faculty" of imagination. Brit. J. Psych. Mon. Suppl. 1927, 3, No. 10.

61. HARLOW, H. F. Thinking (Theoretical Foundations of Psychology, ed. H. Helson) N.Y.: Van Nostrand, 1951.

62. HARROWER, M. R. Organization in higher mental processes. Psych. Forsch. 1932, 17, 56–120.

63. HARTMANN, G. *Educational Psychology.* N.Y.: American Book, 1941.

64. HARTMANN, G. Insight vs. trial and error in the solution of problems. Am. J. Psych. 1933, 45, 663–77.

65. HAZLITT, V. Children's thinking. Brit. J. Psych. 1929–30, 20, 354–61.

66. HEIDBREDER, E. Toward a dynamic psychology of cognition. Psy. Rev. 1945, 52, 1–23.

67. HELMHOLTZ, H. VON. *Vortrage und Reden.* 5th Aufl. Braunschweig f. Vieweg. u. Sohn, 1896.

68. HENDERSON, A. Science and art. Amer. Scient. 1946, 34, 452–63.

69. HENRY, L. K. The role of insight in the analytic thinking of adolescents. Univ. Iowa Stud. Educ. 1934, 9, 65–102.

70. HOLLINGWORTH, H. L. *Educational Psychology.* N.Y.: Appleton, 1933.

71. HOLLINGWORTH, H. L. *The Psychology of Thought.* N.Y.: Appleton, 1927.

72. HORNEY, K. Inhibitions in work. Amer. J. Psychoanal. 1947, 7, 18–25.

73. HOUSMAN, A. E. *The Name and Nature of Poetry.* N.Y.: Macmillan, 1933.

74. HULBRECK, C. R. The creative personality. Amer. J. Psychoanal. 1945, 5, 49–58.

75. HULL, C. L. Trial and error. Psych. Rev. 1930, 37, 241–56.

76. HULL, C. L. Quantitative aspects of the evolution of concepts. Psych. Mon. 1928, 20.

77. HUMPHREY, G. *Thinking.* N.Y.: Wiley, 1951.

78. HUMPHREY, G. *Directed Thinking.* N.Y.: Dodd Mead, 1948.

79. HUMPHREY, G. Problem of direction of thought. Brit. J. Psych. 1940, 30, 183–96.

80. HUTCHINSON, E. D. *How to Think Creatively.* N.Y.: Abingdon-Cokesbury Press, 1949.

81. HUTCHINSON, E. D. The period of elaboration in creative endeavor. Psychiatry, 1942, 5, 165–76.

82. HUTCHINSON, E. D. Nature of insight. Psychiatry, 1941, 4, 31–43.

83. HUTCHINSON, E. D. Period of frustration in creative endeavor. Psychiatry, 1940, 3, 351–9.
84. HUTCHINSON, E. D. Materials for the study of creative thinking. Psych. Bull. 1931, 28, 392–410.
85. ISRAELI, N. Studies in occupational analysis: II. Originality. J. Psych. 1946, 22, 77–87.
86. JAMES, W. *Psychology-Briefer Course.* N.Y.: Holt, 1892.
87. JASTROW, J. *The Subconscious.* N.Y.: Houghton-Mifflin, 1906.
88. JOHNSON, D. M. A modern account of problem-solving. Psych. Bull. 1944, 41, 201–29.
89. KEYES, K. S. *How to Develop Your Thinking Ability.* N.Y.: McGraw-Hill, 1950.
90. KOFFKA, K. *Principles of Gestalt Psychology.* N.Y.: Harcourt Brace, 1935.
91. KOFFKA, K. Mental Development. (Psychologies of 1925, ed. C. Murchison) Worcester: Clark Univ. Press, 1928.
92. KOHLER, W. *Gestalt Psychology.* N.Y.: Liveright, 1947.
93. KRIS, E. On inspiration. Int. J. Psychoanal. 1939, 20, 377–89.
94. KUO, Z. Y. A behavioristic experiment on inductive inference. J. Exp. Psych. 1923, 6, 247–93.
95. LANGFELD, H. S. The Role of Feeling and Emotion in Aesthetics, (The Wittenberg Symposium) Worcester: Clark Univ. Press 1928.
96. LEFFORD, A. The influence of emotional subject matter on logical reasoning. J. Gen. Psych. 1946, 34, 127–51.
97. LEHMAN, H. C. Some examples of creative achievement during later maturity and old age. J. Soc. Psych., 1949, 30, 49–79.
98. LEHMAN, H. C. Man's most creative years: then and now. Science. 1943, 98, 393–99.
99. LEHMAN, H. C. Optimum years for leadership. Sci. Mon. 1942, 54, 162–75.
100. LEHMAN, H. C. and GAMERTSFELDER, W. S. Man's creative years in philosophy. Psych. Rev. 1942, 49, 319–43.
101. LEHMAN, H. C. The creative years: oil paintings, etchings, and architectural works. Psych. Rev. 1942, 49, 18–42.
102. LEHMAN, H. C. The creative years: medicine, surgery, and certain related fields. Sci. Mon. 1941, 59, 450–62.
103. LEHMAN, H. C. The chronological ages of some recipients of large annual incomes. Social Forces, 1941, 20, 196–206.
104. LEHMAN, H. C. and INGERHAM, D. W. Man's creative years in music. Sci. Mon. 1939, 48, 431–43.
105. LEHMAN, H. C. The creative years: best books. Sci. Mon. 1937, 45, 65–75.

106. LEHMAN, H. C. Creative years in science and literature. Sci. Mon. 1936, 43, 151–62.

107. LEWIN, K. Das Problem der Willensmessung und das Grundgesetz der Assoziation. Psych. Forsch. 1922, I, 191–302, II, 65–140.

108. LONG, L. and WELCH, L. Reasoning ability in young children. J. Psych. 1941, 12, 21–44.

109. LONG, L. and WELCH, L. Influence of levels of abstractness on reasoning ability. J. Psych. 1942, 13, 41–59.

110. LOWENFELD, V. *Nature of Creative Activity.* N.Y.: Harcourt Brace, 1939.

111. LOWES, J. L. *Road to Xanadu.* N.Y.: Houghton Mifflin Co. 1930.

112. LUZZATTO, G. L. *Dialoghi su la Creazione Artistica.* Lanciano: 1932.

113. McANDREW, M. B. An experimental investigation of young children's ideas of causality. Stud. Psych. Psychiat. Cathol. Univ. Amer. 1943, 6, No. 2.

114. McCLOY, W. Creative imagination in children and adults. Psych. Mon. 1939, 51, No. 231.

115. MAIER, N. R. F. Reasoning in humans. III. The mechanisms of equivalent stimuli and of reasoning. J. Exp. Psych. 1945, 35, 349–60.

116. MAIER, N. R. F. Reasoning in rats and human beings. Psych. Rev. 1937, 44, 365–78.

117. MAIER, N. R. F. Reasoning and learning. Psych. Rev. 1931, 38, 332–46.

118. MAIER, N. R. F. Reasoning in humans. J. Comp. Psych. 1930, 10, 114–140.

119. MARKEY, F. V. Imagination. Psych. Bull. 1935, 32, 212–36.

120. MATHESON, E. A study of problem solving behavior in preschool children. Child Devlpm. 1931, 2, 242–62.

121. MEARNS, H. *Creative Youth.* N.Y.: Doubleday Doran, 1927.

122. MEIER, N. C. and McCLOY, W. Recreative imagination. Psych. Mon. 1939, 51, No. 231.

123. MEILI, R. La pensee productrice d'apres Claparede et d'apres Duncker. J. de Psych. 1936, 33, 614–28.

124. MEINICKE, G. Einige technische Konstruktionsaufgaben und deren Losungsmethod. Arch. f. d. ges. Psych. 1934, 92, 249–54.

125. MILLER, I. E. *The Psychology of Thinking.* N.Y.: Macmillan, 1909.

126. MOORE, T. V. *Reasoning Ability of Children in the First Years of Life.* Baltimore: Williams, Wilkins, 1929.

127. MORGAN, C. L. Characteristics of problem-solving behavior of adults. Univ. Iowa Stud. Educ. 1934, No. 5.

128. MORRIS, B. *The Aesthetic Process.* Evanston: Northwestern Univ. Press, 1943.

129. MOSSMAN, L. C. *The Activity Concept.* N.Y.: Macmillan, 1938.

130. MURPHY, G. The freeing of intelligence. Psych. Bull. 1945, 42, 1–19.

131. NELSON, H. The creative years. Am. J. Psych. 1948, 61, 303–11.

132. OGDEN, R. M. Insight. Am. J. Psych. 1932, 44, 350–6.

133. OGDEN, R. M. *Psychology and Education.* N.Y.: Harcourt Brace, 1926.

134. OLDFIELD, R. C. and ZANGWILL, O. L. Wolter's theory of thinking. Brit. J. Psych. 1943, 34, 143–9.

135. PARKER, S. C. *Methods of Teaching in High Schools.* N.Y.: Ginn, 1915.

136. PATRICK, C. Creative thought in poets. Arch. Psych. 1935, No. 178.

137. PATRICK, C. Creative thought in artists. J. Psych. 1937, 4, 35–73.

138. PATRICK, C. Scientific thought. J. Psych. 1938, 5, 55–83.

139. PATRICK, C. Whole and part relationship in creative thought. Am. J. Psych. 1941, 54, 128–31.

140. PATRICK, C. Creative thinking. (Encyclopedia of Psychology, ed. P. L. Harriman) N.Y. Phil. Lib. 1946.

141. PAULHAN, F. *Psychologie de l'Invention.* Paris: Alcan, 1901.

142. PECHSTEIN, L. A. and BROWN, F. D. An experimental analysis of the alleged criteria of insight learning. J. Educ. Psych. 1939, 30, 38–52.

143. PELIKAN, A. G. *The Art of the Child.* N.Y.: Bruce, 1931.

144. PIAGET, J. *Judgment and Reasoning in the Child.* N.Y.: Harcourt Brace, 1928.

145. PILLSBURY, W. B. *The Psychology of Reasoning.* N.Y.: Appleton, 1910.

146. PLATT, W. and BAKER, R. A. Relation of the scientific "hunch" to research. J. Chem. Educ. 1931, 8, 1969–2002.

147. POINCARE, H. *The Foundations of Science.* Trans. by G. B. Halsted. Lancaster: Science Press, 1946.

148. POINCARE, H. *Science and Method.* N.Y.: Nelson, 1914.

149. PORTNOY, J. A. *Psychology of Art Creation.* Philadelphia: Univ. Penn. Press, 1942.

150. PRATT, C. C. Experimental studies of thought and reasoning. Psych. Bull. 1928, 25, 550–559.

151. PRESCOTT, F. C. *The Poetic Mind.* N.Y.: Macmillan, 1922.

152. PRESSY, S. L. A neglected crucial psychoeducational problem. J. Psych. 1944, 18, 217–34.

153. PYLE, W. H. *The Psychology of Learning.* Baltimore: Warwick, York. 1928.

154. RAPAPORT, D. *Organization and Pathology of Thought.* N.Y.: Columbia Univ. Press, 1951.

155. REES, H. E. *A Psychology of Artistic Creation.* N.Y.: Columbia, Teach. Coll. Bur. Pub. 1942.

156. REES, H. J. and ISRAEL, H. E. An investigation of the establishment and operation of mental sets. Psych. Mon. 1935, 46, 210.

157. REVESZ, G. Die Psychologie der schoepfenschen Arbeit, Universitas, 1949, 5, 1179–86.

158. RIBOT, T. *Essay on the Creative Imagination.* Chicago: Open Court, 1906.

159. RICE, P. B. The ego and the law of effect. Psych. Rev. 1946, 53, 307–20.

160. RIGNANO, E. *The Psychology of Reasoning.* N.Y.: Harcourt Brace, 1927.

161. ROSETT, J. *The Mechanism of Thought, Imagery, and Hallucination.* N.Y.: Columbia Univ. Press, 1939.

162. ROSSMAN, J. *The Psychology of the Inventor.* Washington: Inventors Pub. Co., 1931.

163. ROYCE, J. The psychology of invention. Psych. Rev. 1898, 5, 113–44.

164. ROYON, A. Construction perceptive et construction logico-arithmetique de la pensee; etude experimental sur la genese de l'invention. Arch. Psych. Geneva, 1940, 28, 81–142.

165. RUCH, F. L. *Psychology and Life.* N.Y.: Scott Foresman, 1941.

166. RUGER, H. A. The psychology of efficiency. Arch. Psych. 1910, 15.

167. SARGENT, S. S. Thinking processes at various levels of difficulty. Arch. Psych. 1940, No. 249.

168. SCHAEFER-SIMMERN, H. *The Unfolding of Artistic Activity.* Berkeley: Univ. Calif. Press, 1948.

169. SCHOEN, M. Creative experience in science and art. J. Aesthet. 1941, 1, 22–32.

170. SELLS, S. B. The atmosphere effect. Arch. Psych. 1936, No. 200.

171. SELZ, O. *Die Gesetze der produktiven und reproduktiven Geistestaligkeit.* Bonn; F. Cohen, 1924.

172. SELZ, O. *Uber die Gesetze des geordneten Denkverlaufs. Eine experimentele Untersuchung.* Stuttgart: W. Spemann, 1913.

173. SEWARD, G. H. and SEWARD, J. P. Alcohol and task complexity. Arch. Psych. 1936, No. 206.

174. SHAFFER, L. F., GILMER, B. von H., and SCHOEN, M. *Psychology.* N.Y.: Harper, 1940.

175. SIIPOLA, E. M. A group study of some effects of preparatory set. Psych. Mon. 1935, 46, 210.

176. SMOKE, K. L. Experimental approach to concept learning. Psych. Rev. 1935, 42, 274–9.

177. SNYDER, E. D. *Hypnotic Poetry.* Philadelphia: Univ. Penn. Press, 1930.

178. SPEARMAN, C. *Creative Mind.* N.Y.: Appleton, 1931.

179. STERN, W. *General Psychology.* N.Y.: Macmillan, 1938.

180. STORRING, G. Experimentelle Untersuchungen über Einfache Schlussprozesse. Arch. f. d. ges. Psych. 1908, 11, 1–127.

181. SUCHODOLSKI, B. Krytyka Piageta w. psychologie radzieckiej. Psych. Wychow. 1949, 14, 18–22.

182. SYMONDS, P. M. *Education and the Psychology of Thinking.* N.Y.: McGraw-Hill, 1936.

183. Symposium on thinking: BARTLETT, F. C. and SMITH, E. M.; THOMSON, G. H.; PEAR, T. H.; ROBINSON, A.; WATSON, J. B. Brit. J. Psych. 1920, 11, 55–104.

184. Symposium on the psychology of music and painting. WHITTAKER, G.; HUTCHISON, W. O.; and PICKFORD, R. W. Brit. J. Psych. 1942, 33, 40–57.

185. SZEKELY, L. Knowledge and thinking. Acta Psych. 1950, 7, 1–24.

186. THORNDIKE, E. L. The psychology of invention in a very simple case. Psych. Rev. 1949, 56, 192–99.

187. THORNDIKE, E. L. *Human Learning.* N.Y.: Century, 1931.

188. THORNDIKE, E. L. Effect of changed data on reasoning. J. Exp. Psych. 1922, 5, 33–38.

189. THURSTONE, L. L. Creative talent. Proc. 1950 Conf. Test. Probl., Educ. Test Serv. 1951, 55–69.

190. TRAMER, M. Creatismus (Sofia: Padova) 1941, 9, 20–33.

191. UNDERWOOD, B. J. An orientation for research on thinking. Psych. Rev. 1952, 59, 209–20.

192. VINACKE, W. E. *The Psychology of Thinking.* N.Y.: McGraw-Hill, 1951.

193. WALLAS, G. *The Art of Thought.* N.Y.: Harcourt Brace, 1926.
194. WARREN, H. C. and CARMICHAEL, L. *Elements of Human Psychology.* N.Y.: Houghton, Mifflin, 1930.
195. WATT, H. J. Experimentelle Beitrage zu einer Theorie des Denkens. Arch. f. d. Ges. Psych. 1905, 4, 289–436.
196. WEINLAND, C. E. Creative thought in scientific research. Sci. Mon. 1952, 75, 350–54.
197. WEISSKOPF, E. Some comments concerning the role of education in the "creation of creation." Amer. Psych. 1950, 5, 346–7.
198. WERTHEIMER, M. *Productive Thinking,* N.Y.: Harper, 1945.
199. WERTHEIMER, M. *Drei Abhandlungen zu Gestalttheorie,* Erlangen, 1925.
200. WERTHEIMER, M. *Uber Schlussprozesse im produktiven Denken.* Erlangen, 1920.
201. WHEELER, R. H. *Science of Psychology.* N.Y.: Crowell, 1940.
202. WHEELER, R. H. *Readings in Psychology.* N.Y.: Crowell, 1939.
203. WHEELER, R. H. *Laws of Human Nature.* N.Y.: Appleton, 1932.
204. WILKINS, M. G. The effect of changed material on ability to do formal syllogistic reasoning. Arch. Psych. 1928, No. 16.
205. WILLMANN, R. R. An experimental investigation of the creative process in music. Psych. Mon. 1944, 57, No. 261.
206. WITTY, P. Creative writing in the elementary school. Schoolmens Wk. Proceed. 1942, 29, 127–135.
207. WOODWORTH, R. S. *Experimental Psychology.* N.Y.: Holt, 1938.
208. WOODWORTH, R. S. *Psychology: A Study of Mental Life.* N.Y.: Holt, 1921.
209. YERKES, R. M. The mind of a gorilla. Genet. Psych. Mon. 1937, 2.

INDEX